ALSO BY BOBBY HUNDREDS

This Is Not a T-Shirt

NFTS ARE A SCAM
NFTS ARE THE FUTURE

NFTS
ARE A
SCAM

FUTURE
ARE THE
NFTS

THE EARLY YEARS: 2020–2023

BOBBY HUNDREDS

MCD FARRAR, STRAUS AND GIROUX • NEW YORK

MCD
Farrar, Straus and Giroux
120 Broadway, New York 10271

Bomb illustrations from Adam Bomb Squad and Badam Bomb Squad.

Library of Congress Control Number: 2023000436
ISBN: 978-0-374-61029-6

Designed by Gretchen Achilles

Our books may be purchased in bulk for promotional, educational,
or business use. Please contact your local bookseller or the Macmillan
Corporate and Premium Sales Department at 1-800-221-7945, extension
5442, or by email at MacmillanSpecialMarkets@macmillan.com.

www.mcdbooks.com • www.fsgbooks.com
Follow us on Twitter, Facebook, and Instagram at @mcdbooks

10 9 8 7 6 5 4 3 2 1

For the Squad

CONTENTS

Prologue   3

NFTs Are a Scam   13

NFTs Are a Revolution   45

NFTs Are Fashion   53

NFTs Are Streetwear   75

NFTs Are Culture   87

NFTs Are Religion   109

The Street Does Not Really Exist   135

The Hardest Year   155

NFTs Are Forever   235

NFTs Aren't Dead   245

Epilogue: NFTs Are the Future   267

    Frequently Asked Questions   275

    Acknowledgments   289

NFTS ARE A SCAM
NFTS ARE THE FUTURE

PROLOGUE

*Many people I know in Los Angeles believe that
the Sixties ended abruptly on August 9, 1969, at
the exact moment when word of the murders on
Cielo Drive traveled like brushfire through the
community, and in a sense this is true. The tension broke that day. The paranoia was fulfilled.*

—JOAN DIDION, *THE WHITE ALBUM*

Just one week before Woodstock, the summer music festival that symbolized the sixties love and peace movement, the hippie cult leader Charles Manson directed four
of his disciples to brutally murder the pregnant actress
Sharon Tate and four other victims. The Manson family
murders (along with the Altamont concert stabbing several months later) closed the chapter on an era defined by
daisies, VWs, and long hair. The hippies had a good thing
going, resisting the constraints of American social mores,
dropping out of conventional careers, and practicing free
love and liberal drug experimentation. Critics, however,
deemed their antiestablishment attitudes as solicitation

of social decay and immorality. In her essay "Slouching Towards Bethlehem," the writer Joan Didion zeroes in on the dark side of the culture fomenting around Haight and Ashbury in that decade. From her perspective, hippies were less about revolution and more about aimless runaways, rampant LSD abuse, and societal atomization. Manson and his devotees were the worst possible outcome of the socially disjointed, shapeless hippie way of life.

To be fair, Charles Manson wasn't a hippie at all. He was a criminal that had spent more than half of his life in prison before his release in 1967, whereupon he preyed on and manipulated young women to join his clan through drugs and orgies. Although the hippie movement professed positive and progressive ideals, it also exposed the naive and overly trusting to dark predators. In a *Vice* interview, the Columbia professor Joshua Furst says, "From 1966 to 1969, there was a conscious attempt by counterculture leaders to attempt to break down the existing social structures and find some better contract between human beings . . . Peace and love was the obvious thing, but peace and love is vague and abstract—and that's the issue. The late-sixties counterculture stripped away old systems of control and opened up a blank space in society, but they weren't sure what would fill that space. And Manson preyed on that ambiguity."

For the last few years, I've been immersed in Web3, an umbrella term for the next internet that is based on NFTs, the Metaverse, and blockchain ownership. When I entered in 2020, Web3 was a hopeful and idealistic space for crypto bros, artists, and futurists who pictured a better world for all. NFTs could help struggling artists bypass the gatekeepers, the Metaverse might give people the opportunity to be their most honest selves, and smart contracts should make for more efficient exchanges. Soon, much of mainstream culture also shared a curiosity, if not enthusiasm, for what Web3 could bring.

At the close of 2021, the *Collins English Dictionary* selected "NFT" as Word of the Year. This was the exclamation mark on a sensational twelve months that witnessed over $40 billion in cryptocurrency transactions (surpassing traditional art sales), the artist Beeple's $69 million Christie's auction, "JPEG Summer" led by Bored Ape Yacht Club (BAYC), and Nike's acquisition of metaverse fashion brand RTFKT. Just between Q2 and Q3 of 2021, NFT trading increased by 700 percent.

By the end of 2022, however, a downward economy and crypto slump took the wind out of the NFT market. In late spring, the Terra Luna crash vaporized $45 billion worth of crypto in a couple days, destabilizing the entire industry. The final blow was the collapse of FTX, a cryptocurrency exchange that, once valued at $32 billion, filed for bankruptcy in November. FTX's thirty-year-old founder, Sam Bankman-Fried, was arrested in the Bahamas and extradited to the U.S. on fraud and money laundering charges. He was accused of stealing billions of dollars of his clients' money (and losing it), and U.S. Attorney for the Southern District of New York Damian Williams called SBF's offense one of the largest financial frauds in American history. In fact, we've yet to grasp the enormity of the devastation as the investigation continues and the trial has yet to begin. Everyday investors have had their lives upturned, but it's theorized that the ramifications will tear not just across crypto but the global economy. At the least, mainstream sentiment toward crypto has been muted if not obliterated since the scandal. It seems likely that Bankman-Fried's swindle will continue to leave a bitter aftertaste around the crypto conversation for years to come.

And yet Web3 continues to thrive in the shadows beyond the bright circle of the spotlight. Not only does money continue to pour into the ecosystem, but artists, entrepreneurs, and brands haven't stopped innovating in the space. In 2023, corporations like Starbucks, Nike, and Amazon are set to plant deeper flags in digital collectibles and blockchain-backed rewards programs. And although traditional NFT brands like Bored Ape Yacht Club continue to sell out (in January 2023, BAYC yielded over 4,000 ETH [over $6 million] in total sales volume within hours of releasing their Sewer Pass collection), NFTs are expanding beyond speculative digital assets and being more thoughtfully utilized as membership cards, fandom badges, and tickets. The current trend is to jettison the word altogether and rebrand NFTs as "digital collectibles." The reality is that visionaries, artists, and cash-grabbing opportunists never stopped throwing their entire weight behind Web3, and the ones that remain are doubling down. NFTs and the Metaverse are still early in the process of being defined, legitimized, and proven. The core creators and collectors believe that the journey has only just begun.

That's because NFTs embody more than the million-dollar cartoons that the media depicts them to be. There are tremors of a cultural revolution rattling. Artists are circumventing the traditional gatekeepers and partaking in royalties for their work. Corporations are being decentralized, the brands being governed by their communities. And society is assigning financial value and ownership to digital property in a way that is transactable and records provenance. We've never seen anything like it before.

NFTs Are a Scam / NFTs Are the Future is a time capsule, a snapshot of us as we sit between worlds: Web2 versus Web3. Prepandemic versus postpandemic. Doubt versus belief. (I'm as much a skeptic as an early adopter and so I'll be reporting from both sides.) *NFTs Are a Scam / NFTs Are the Future* is based on a series of essays that I wrote on the subject from 2021 to 2022. Disclaimer: Yesterday's facts are today's fables. I'm cognizant that there are ideas that haven't aged well. The space and innovation are moving faster than any technology paradigm shift in history, so there are plenty of thoughts I got wrong or that died on the vine. Having said that, look beyond the text. In these essays, I'm not just explaining the technology, but documenting attitudes, culture, and the truth behind who we are at this juncture in time. Somewhere between the lines, I believe there's a reason this is all happening.

Joan Didion was wrong.* She missed the forest for the trees and was likely influenced by the media's negative depiction of the sixties counterculture. The hippie movement wasn't inherently evil or bankrupt, although bad actors did exploit its fissures. Furthermore, Charles Manson and his followers went on a murderous spree, but the

---

* In *The New Yorker*, Louis Menand writes, "In 1967, when Didion's article came out, only one per cent of college students reported having tried LSD. In 1969, only four per cent of adults said they had smoked marijuana."

hippie movement never died. The term dissipated in a puff of smoke, but hippie ideals planted deep roots for environmentalism, marijuana legalization, natural foods, and revised attitudes around sexuality. Just look at modern technology. Steve Jobs and Steve Wozniak were hippies whose personal computing machines channeled beliefs of antiauthoritarianism and nonconformity. "Here's to the crazy ones. The misfits. The rebels. The troublemakers. The round pegs in the square holes."

Half a century later, the hippies have won the culture wars, when you scan music, social justice, and even the psychedelics renaissance in treating mental health disorders. Another by-product of the hippie worldview? Web3. And like the hippies, Web3 participants will continue to exist, whether in mainstream culture or relegated to a subculture. You can lay "NFTs" to rest at SBF's sentencing, but my bet is that Web3's principles will inspire and affect culture for generations to come.

Much like the space in the span of these two years, I use the words "crypto," "NFTs," "the Metaverse," and "Web3" liberally and, at times, interchangeably. It's important that you understand, however, that they are distinct concepts and, in many ways, exist on different planes.

"Crypto" is short for "cryptocurrency," which is a relatively new form of digital, decentralized currency.* It's not "fiat" money that is government-issued and backed by a commodity like gold (think the U.S. dollar or Japanese

---

* There are many different cryptocurrencies, including the one that started it all: Bitcoin. In addition to SOL (Solana) and MATIC (Polygon), Ether (ETH) is the most popular crypto for NFTs and is built atop the Ethereum blockchain.

NFTS ARE A SCAM

yen). With cryptocurrencies like Bitcoin, you can send and receive value with someone directly over the internet without having to go through a centralized corporation like a bank. There is no middleman. Crypto isn't just about money, however. It's a culture that houses NFTs and the Metaverse. It's also a philosophy that challenges and subverts many of the systems we participate in today, like finance, government, and art.

"NFTs" stands for "non-fungible tokens," which are essentially records of property and assets on the blockchain. Kind of like a house deed or an art certificate. This property can be digital art in the form of JPEGs, which is the most mainstream representation of NFTs today.* When I talk about "NFTs" in this book, I will almost always be referring to the "PFP" variety, which is probably the same kind you're thinking about (million-dollar cartoon animals). "PFP" stands for "profile picture" because collectors use them as their social media avatars to express identity and tribal associations.

It is important, however, to understand that NFTs can also refer to one-of-one art (think of precious paintings), music, digital fashion, and membership cards for subscription services.† These are all wholly different things with their own values, expectations, and rules. Unfortunately, "NFT" is used as a blanket description across all these assets and services, and it's caused massive confusion and frustration among its participants. You don't think of a Picasso painting the same way you would a loy-

---

* An NFT can also be a receipt documenting ownership of *physical* goods.
† Also important: don't conflate NFTs with the art itself.

alty rewards card or a streetwear T-shirt. They are sold in different places, have different purposes, and carry different values. Today, in Web3, they're are all rolled together as "NFTs."

The Metaverse is essentially a repackaged offering of *Second Life*, video games, and virtual reality (VR), which has been pursued for decades. Many founders and companies are building metaverses, which collectively comprise the Metaverse with a capital "M." The top examples of modern metaverses are *Roblox*, *Fortnite*, and Meta's *Horizon Worlds*. The Metaverse is lumped into the crypto conversation is because companies are working on making assets interoperable among devices and applications. An illustration of this would be if you could wear your *NBA 2K* Nike sneakers—that you own—as an Instagram filter. To achieve this, the sneakers would have to be NFTs that are registered to you on a universal blockchain.

Web3 is the umbrella term for this new iteration of the internet where users can have and track ownership of digital assets. Web2 loosely covered the social media era of Facebook and Instagram, whereby Big Tech accumulated disproportionate amounts of wealth off its users' content. Web3 seeks to repair that exchange through decentralizing power and ownership.

Finally, breaking down the blockchain would take an entire book. Without getting into the granular details, imagine a network of computers around the world all having to come into agreement with one another (consensus) to determine fact. Once set in place, to disassemble that truth would be nearly impossible, requiring unraveling the record one computer at a time. It's a rigid, foolproof system in an era where everything is liquid, Photoshoppable, and relative.

What brought me into this world of NFTs were their art, culture, and community components—all languages I love and speak daily. But there are many doors to enter this room. You can walk in as a trader or a flipper. You can be a patron of the arts, a venture capitalist, or a scammer. Among other things, my Web3 journey has been inspired by equitable systems for artists, potential for wealth parity, better means of community building, and a reformation of the brand-consumer relationship. My last book, *This Is Not a T-Shirt*, chronicled the story of our streetwear label, The Hundreds, and how we built a brand around community. *NFTs Are a Scam / NFTs Are the Future* is about what happens when the community builds the brand. However, this book shouldn't be taken as infallible truth. It's far from being perfect and permanent—like the blockchain! Instead, it should be used to provoke dialogue and new ideas. When it comes to NFTs, we're all building the definition, in real time, together.

In the meantime, here's what I think . . .

NFTS ARE A SCAM

After Trump left office, America found itself on two sides of a gorge. It wasn't solely Donald's fault that our nation became so split (we can also thank social media, wealth disparity, a global pandemic, etc.), but four years of his polarizing presidency exacerbated a deep divide between ideological tribes. So much so that once Biden took the wheel many Americans didn't know where to direct their passions. Trumpers were lost without a leader, but his haters may have been even more disoriented. My neighbor Tim's entire identity throughout the Trump administration was to grumble about the president's tweets and mishaps, but after the election he was rocked off-center. It was like watching a boxer roam aimlessly around the ring alone, swinging at GameStop stonks and anti-vaxxers. Just days after Biden's inauguration, Tim approached me as I was taking out the trash.

"You know what I don't get about NFTs?" He had been reading my tweets.

"What's that?" I asked.

"Why would you buy something that you can't hold? Look, I get art. If I want to buy a painting, I want it in my hands and on my wall. But I can just screen-grab an NFT. People are idiots for paying so much money for them."

I chuckled and shrugged. I thought Tim was just trying to make small talk, so I turned to walk back up my driveway.

"No, really!" he shouted after me. "It's such a gimmick. The new Pet Rock!"

Tim wasn't asking for clarification. He was demanding an answer. The NFT thing was bothering him, and as the months went by and I delved deeper into the space, his ire grew.

"My PlayStation One had better graphics than the Metaverse!"

"Did you see Seth Green got his Bored Ape stolen? What's he gonna do now?"

"I heard that NFTs can change. I thought the blockchain was forever!"

NFTs were the new Trump and Tim wasn't the only dissident. His jabs mirrored the comments and DMs in my Instagram feed. Whenever I'd publish anything related to NFTs, hecklers would swarm my account, ridiculing me for promoting crypto and threatening to unfollow me "after all these years." I wasn't even mad about it. I was intrigued. NFTs started getting so popular and so noisy so fast that it fanned the flames from critics and trolls. To take the piss out of the tension, we printed The Hundreds

T-shirts that read "NFTS ARE A SCAM" and also posted the statement on a digital billboard in the center of Times Square. During NFT.NYC week, we staged a protest in front of our New York pop-up shop. We hired Craigslist actors to march with signs that read "GOD HATES NFTS," "MAKE FIAT GREAT AGAIN," and "REPENT OR GET RUGGED." The video went viral across TikTok and other meme sites. Of course, most of the likes and comments were by people who didn't get the joke and sympathized with the anti-NFT sentiments. In the spring of 2022, once the market turned bearish, we printed "NFTS ARE DEAD" hoodies and the reactions were priceless. Wearing that sweatshirt through the airport brought so much joy and schadenfreude to travelers.

"Right on! Fuck NFTs!"

"I just wanted to say, man, I love your sweatshirt. They're such a scam."

From an anthropological stance, the fact that the topic of NFTs was eliciting such a visceral response was almost more interesting than NFTs themselves. This went beyond tribalism and side-picking. NFTs were making people uncomfortable. Perhaps they made people feel stupid or irrelevant. Maybe cynics felt like they were being left behind while all their friends were making money. It's also possible that they felt like the only noncrazy ones. Whenever the issue was broached at dinner parties, I could see the disgust wash over people's faces like they'd eaten a bad oyster. Half the table was amused by the conversation. The other half would leave for the bar.

We've survived so much tumult and disorder over the last several years that many of us just want the ground to stop shaking. After all the mandates, the illnesses, the racial strife, and gender debates, the last thing some people want is to hear that we're going full *Ready Player One* on their ass. The majority of people don't understand how the art, stock, or vintage markets work as far as trading and secondhand sales go. Yet here we are trying to force digital versions of those assets down their throats. Of course they're gonna barf.

Whether or not NFTs are a scam poses a philosophical question that wanders into moral judgments and cultural practices around free enterprise, mercantilism, and materialism. If NFTs are a scam, what about the blue-chip art galleries and auction houses that charge millions of dollars for oils on canvas? What about mass-produced Air Jordans that fetch thousands of dollars on reselling sites—and they're not even used to play basketball? If crypto is corrupt, what about the U.S. financial system that continues to benefit the rich and disenfranchise the poor? What about the ruthless throes of capitalism itself?

In 1944's *The Great Transformation*, the Hungarian American political economist Karl Polanyi contends that some commodities, like land and human labor, are entirely concocted to be bought and sold on the market. What's worse, it's morally wrong to put price tags on these things when they should remain public goods and necessities to live. If we leave it up to the market to determine their value, the ramifications for humankind can be devastating. Fred Block summarizes Polanyi's thoughts: "Polanyi insists that this sleight of hand has fatal consequences. It means that economic theorizing is based on a lie, and this lie places human society at risk." Money is the third of these "lies" that Polanyi zeroes in on. "Money ... is merely a token of purchasing power which, as a rule, is not produced at all, but comes into being through the mechanism of banking or state finance."

I don't disagree with Polanyi. Many commodities begin as myths, fictions, and lies but then they become normalized and deeply embedded in our social experience. Nowadays, it's customary to pay for land, hire labor, and exchange money without a second thought of these transactions being based on completely fabricated phenomena. So much changed over time in order for land to be considered ownable and labor to be more than "the human beings themselves of which every society consists." Polanyi would've abhorred the idea of crypto and NFTs, but only time will tell how broadly they'll be adopted and normalized in the years to come.

So, are NFTs a scam? Or are they just new?

There are two faces to radical technology, and the hopeful future promised by crypto and Web3 is undergirded by controversy. For one, there are dire environmental concerns around the methods by which cryptocurrency is mined. The United States mines over a third of the Bitcoin in the world, creating over forty billion pounds of carbon dioxide alone. Globally, Bitcoin's CO_2 emissions are the equivalent of energy used by 2.6 to 2.7 billion homes in one year. There are even studies that suggest Bitcoin could push global warming beyond 2°C.

Another cause for concern: Like any technological

upheaval and nascent marketplace, Web3 is fertile ground for bad actors and scams. Crypto is assembling at light speed, so the opportunity for rapid wealth is bountiful. That also means there are ample ways to be drained, "rugged," and scammed. Since the creative conversations and ideation are outpacing the infrastructure (facilitated by town squares like Twitter and Discord), the systems are being built hastily, resulting in flimsy and porous scaffolding, exposing security holes and vulnerabilities. Factor in the snake oil salespeople, the anonymity, the froth and hype, and the lack of education and regulation in the space, and it's a perfect storm of swindling.

If you're predisposed to hating NFTs because of the scamming connotations, there are plenty of reasons to support your position. Since July of 2021, more than $100 million worth of NFTs have been stolen, primarily through phishing scams where NFT owners are duped into handing over the keys to their wallets.* In the spring of 2022, North Korean hackers plundered a half billion dollars from the NFT-based video game Axie Infinity. Even Kim Kardashian was penalized $1.2 million by the SEC for promoting "pump-and-dump" crypto scams on her Instagram. It's no surprise, then, that NFTs are often called out as gambling, Ponzis, and pyramid schemes

---

* For example, an anonymous scammer entered our (The Hundreds') Discord at three in the morning and fooled our community, claiming that we were surprise-minting a second Adam Bomb Squad collection. Within half an hour, they convinced our holders to fork over $100,000 for bootleg NFTs before our moderators woke us up and we could regain control of the room. Because crypto is decentralized, meaning there is no government or central authority involved, the money vanished into thin air.

propagated by cutthroat day traders, avaricious capitalists, and con artists.

NFTs have blown up so quickly and with such little understanding and footing that they beg suspicion and disbelief. From 2021 to 2022, the number of NFT collections went from fifteen thousand to over eighty thousand.* By mid-2022, there were hundreds of thousands (if not millions) of NFT collectors, trading volume over $54 billion. To a doubter or critic, that's a lot of money associated with JPEGs that anyone can just right-click and save to their desktops for free. In fact, when your brain plugs into the Matrix, you realize that NFTs are just a string of letters and numbers (hash token), coded on the blockchain. So, the monetary value of the NFTs has nothing to do with the virtual asset itself. What makes these NFTs worth so much money rides on the same question regarding value as any other art, novelty, or collectible.

Unlike NFTs, many physical goods have obvious, inherent utility and much of their worth is baked into their functionality. There's little debate that a hammer should be exchanged for money because the purpose and usefulness are apparent and socially agreed upon. A cup of coffee can be overpriced, but we rationalize its cost by how

---

* The first NFTs in the late 2010s were blockchain experiments for a handful of engineers and artists around the world. But during the pandemic, interest in NFTs skyrocketed as people were locked down at home and transitioning most of their waking hours to the internet. After RAC sold a $13,000 NFT redeemable for a physical cassette tape of his music, the artist Beeple made millions auctioning digital art, NBA Top Shot introduced digital collectibles to the sports card collectors, and Hashmasks proved that anyone could copy the CryptoPunks model, thousands of founders seized the opportunity to participate in the new gold rush.

delicious or effective it is in waking us up. However, when the same logic is applied to most JPEGs, their price is impossible to justify since they don't actually "do" anything.* Without any immediate or obvious utility, NFTs can be quickly dismissed as scams or "rugs" (short for "rugpull" and slang for fraud, as in "getting the rug pulled out from under you").

Therefore, the best way to justify value around most current NFTs is by classifying them differently, as art or novelty collectibles. Under this context, price is more plastic, contingent on abstract factors, and has more to do with how the market subjectively perceives it. "Art is in the eye of the beholder." When you buy art, you pay a price that goes beyond the mere materials employed or labor involved in its composition. And there are a multitude of reasons as to why we exchange money for art. Art provides aesthetic enjoyment and entertainment, like music and movies. Since art can be emotional, there's a price we put on that meaningfulness. Fine art can be deemed special due to the artist's significance or the gallery's co-sign. We're not just paying for a pretty picture, we're compensating the sought-after artist for their time, technique, and storytelling. Art, like collectibles, can also have high value because of rarity or exclusivity. The marketing and branding that package the art can increase the art's profile, and therefore the demand and price for it may rise. It can also work the other way around, vis-à-vis Veblen

---

* This almost always then leads to the "Wen utility?" demand (when will the purpose of this NFT be disclosed?) by the project's holders. If they aren't satisfied by the mere collectible nature of the NFT, the holders are of the opinion that it must be a simple ticket or placeholder to receive or accomplish something more substantive down the road.

goods, whereby raising the price of the art may make it more esteemed. This is often what we see with luxury goods or streetwear.*

If NFTs are precious art, however, how to make sense of PFP-style NFT collections where there are ten thousand near duplicates of the same image? And if they are fun, novelty collectibles, why are they trading for colossal amounts of money? In the summer of 2021, NFTs accelerated by virtue of crypto's surge, COVID surplus checks, and a reexamination of traditional systems. Practically overnight, JPEGs were selling for tens—if not hundreds—of thousands of dollars on marketplaces like Bitski and Foundation. The game suddenly went from fun to finance as the professionals (crypto, stocks, blue-chip art) sauntered in and gamified the gambling aspect of NFT mints and reveals. While some NFT collections transcended the fracas and developed into legitimate brands over time, the staggering number of NFTs that quickly turned and burned called the space's integrity, legality, and morality into question.

Football cards, Squishmallow pillows, and exotic cacti all operate off the same rare distribution and collectability principles as NFTs. They experienced reselling booms during the pandemic as well, fetching prices on par with popular NFTs. Yet they weren't dragged or canceled by a vocal majority. People selling classic cars and Nintendo cartridges in their original packaging were making out

* There is little difference between a Supreme hooded sweatshirt and Zara outside of the higher ticket price and brand name. Toyota and Lexus share the same owner and the cars feature many identical attributes, yet are valued differently in the marketplace.

like bandits by selling sheer sentimentality and childhood nostalgia. Meanwhile, NFTs were mocked by Elon Musk and Bill Gates and parodied in an *SNL* skit. Why?

It wasn't the confusing concept or the technical hurdles that hamstrung NFTs in the short years leading up to 2023. In my opinion, more than anything, it was about the astronomical price tags that NFTs were fetching on the reselling sites. If the market had priced NFTs to remain affordable, or at least escalate in value organically, both the scammers and the mainstream opinion may have stayed neutral. Even if skeptics didn't understand how you could own something digital, they would have been more indifferent about the technology if it was a low-risk pastime like collecting gaming skins or in-app purchases. The high prices that NFTs commanded, however, were impossible to leave alone.

The art form's digital nature also lowered the barrier of entry for both creators and collectors to participate. Fairer access is one of Web3's virtues, but for some founders, the overnight success—facilitated by digital interfaces and computer-aided design—implied illegitimate and maybe even unscrupulous means. "Get rich quick." Take, for instance, high-end art. Contemporary paintings and sculptures can go for more than NFTs. Although the general public might not appreciate the art's value the same as a collector ("My kid can paint that"), the sticker is normalized by generations of customs, practices, and industry.

Or how about retro sneakers? They also command absurd bids on the secondary market, but that phenomenon has been cultivated over the course of decades. There were years for the culture and storytelling to foster organically before a halo floated above the vintage product. Also, for the majority of the time only a handful of corporations and retailers profited from sneakers. In NFTs, thousands of everyday folks have gone from "rugs" to riches. Furthermore, they've done it within weeks and months with very little foundation for the art.

The core sticking point against NFTs, however, isn't about their designation as art or even their environmental implications. I don't even think it's because it's a new, bewildering technology or disruptive mindset around art and ownership. It's that something about NFTs feels illicit, like contraband. The government is scrambling to regulate them. The institutions are slow to adapt. The celebrities are afraid of endorsing NFTs because of the vehement hate in the comments. And yet, there are massive amounts of money being transacted around them, which is reminiscent of the black-market drug or sex trades.

Compare NFTs with other collectibles, even the expensive ones. Logan Paul bought his 1998 holographic Pikachu "Illustrator" card for over $5 million and it was written off as a stunt. Over the pandemic, my children became obsessed with trading Pokémon cards, with some selling for hundreds of dollars in the name of fun. However, if they were trading Gengar VMAXes for ETH, the hobby would be taken in a different light and would lose its innocence. That's because crypto continues to carry a stigma as antiestablishment and subversive, even anarchic and insidious.

The primary reason why NFTs are seen as a scam is because they are enmeshed with cryptocurrency. Some critics see crypto as a tool to skirt the system, evade taxes, and wash money. Others consider crypto a speculative bubble, in which the price rises unsustainably and without justifiable reason. At the start of 2022, the YouTuber Dan Olson produced a video called "Line Goes Up—The Problem with NFTs," in which he rails against NFTs for their bad art and tacky, play-to-earn video games. At ten million views, "Line Goes Up" fast became doctrine for the anti-NFT crowd and was covered by *The New York Times*, NPR, and *The Verge*. To this day, commenters on the video thank Olson for effectively killing NFTs, citing the release of his video as the catalyst for the NFT bear market. But "Line Goes Up" wasn't just about NFTs. Olson's driving thesis for why NFTs are problematic is that they are a Trojan horse to dupe more people into adopting cryptocurrencies. Crypto is what truly irks Olson. In his opinion, it's not unlike a multilevel marketing scam whereby 99 percent of participants lose money in a pyramid scheme.

It's hard to refute Olson's claims primarily because . . . in many ways, he's right. Crypto has shady elements. Many—if not most—NFTs really are a wholesale scam and so many of them are purely speculative, grounded in thoughts and prayers. Participating in the NFT collectibles space over the past couple of years, I've witnessed fraudulent collections dominating the conversation with the support of venerable corporations, likable celebrities, and influencers. The money distracts, then it distorts. There's so much easy crypto to be made that branding principles are ignored, long-term business decisions are forsaken, and moral boundaries are smudged. Many of the project leaders who are lauded for making their communities large returns on their investments did so through ethically cloudy practices. Even if a founder has virtuous intentions, the tech and culture are so transparent that you get to see their capitalist motivations on full, naked display.

The softest corner of Web3, to me, is also the one that has had the most money pumped into it: the Metaverse. In the winter of 2021, collectors were buying virtual land from metaverse companies for prices that rivaled physical real estate. This, even when most of these founders and teams admitted that it would be several years before their worlds would be built and operable. One of the companies quoted us (The Hundreds and Adam Bomb Squad) hundreds of thousands of dollars for a plot of digital pixels the size of a virtual basketball court. We were flabbergasted. When they teased a preview of their metaverse weeks later, it was evident that it would be ages before they accomplished their project, if ever. To this day, that specific metaverse is nowhere close to being built and the price for that rectangle of land is in the gutter.

Mark Zuckerberg is facing similar problems over at Meta. The company formerly known as Facebook has lost over $27 billion in operating costs over three years building their own version of the Metaverse. Yet only 58 percent of the staff understand Zuckerberg's metaverse strategy, and he has admitted that the process has taken a lot longer than anticipated. In the fall of 2022, a report estimated that Decentraland, one of the most prominent metaverse companies, had 38 active users a day. Sandbox, a competitor, had 522. (Both Decentraland and

Sandbox have disputed these numbers.) Meanwhile, both companies tout billion-dollar valuations. Another study reported sales for eighteen metaverse companies were down 98 percent from 2021 to 2022.

Whenever NFT criticism arises, the cheeky rebuttal from the crypto community is "We're still early." When NFT influencers are outed for stealing funds: "We're still early." When crypto coins collapse, taking hundreds of millions of investors' dollars with them: "We're still early." When blockchains like Solana periodically crash and go offline: "We're still early." In the early days of 2021, there were rah-rah rallying cries like WAGMI (We're All Gonna Make It) and GM (Good Morning) that spirited the fervent enthusiasm behind Web3 mania. While most of the mantras sank to the bottom of the ocean with the market tides, the sweet and sanguine "We're still early" continues to live on. Because it's the truth. In the grand scope of modern history, the premise of crypto—Web3, NFTs, and the Metaverse—has barely just materialized. Cryptocurrency was invented in 2008. NFTs were invented just a few years ago. We are still incredibly, profoundly early.

Long before NFTs and crypto were invented, whistleblowers were sounding the alarm on another scam: the World Wide Web. Whether it was catfishing or catastrophically failed start-ups like Pets.com, the internet's first days were clunky and rife with duplicity. Most of us thought twice before entering our credit card information, and if we ordered something on eBay, we were mentally prepared to never receive the shipment. If you had an email account in the 2000s, you remember the Nigerian prince scam or the "Nigerian letter."* The phishing email was purported to be delivered by a high-ranking government official or person of royalty from Nigeria, notifying you about a transfer of money in exchange for help. It seems absurd nowadays that anyone would fall for such a blatant scam, but at the time, spam emails like these successfully bamboozled billions of dollars from gullible internet noobs.

In Bill Stewart's early guide to the web, *Living Internet* (published in 1996), he exhorts a strong disclaimer regarding safe email practices:

> Never . . . respond to an email that asks for personal information like a phone number or address, never send money to anyone who contacts you by email for any reason whatsoever, try to never open or preview any unsolicited email, and do not give your email address or anyone else's to any website (news, greeting cards) unless absolutely required and worthwhile.

The admonition is strongly reminiscent of modern-day Web3 disclaimers that accompany Ledger cold wallets, OpenSea navigation, and Discord login pages. Meanwhile, the traditional internet has become so overrun with scams and phishing that we have separate email receptacles to collect junk mail. We're also required to enter a password

---

* The Better Business Bureau reports that the Nigerian letter scam still raked in over $700,000 in 2019.

to unlock our phone, another to access our inbox, which sends a two-factor authentication text back to our phone, so that we can solve a CAPTCHA puzzle, in order to receive an email, which asks to confirm that yes, indeed, we are the ones holding the device. We do this countless times a day on every website and app we use. Yet we still get targeted, manipulated, and even robbed, whether it's by terrorist hackers or Big Tech selling off our data. NFTs are a scam, sure, but so is the internet, so is the world.

The Nigerian letter actually predates email and started in 1989 or 1990 when British businessmen were tricked into paying cash up front for Nigerian crude. In fact, the inspiration for that rugpull originated hundreds of years before in the eighteenth century. With the Spanish prisoner scam, an impostor pretends to be a wealthy, reputable person imprisoned in a Spanish jail under a false identity. The scammer fools the victim to keep paying money to help him out for a variety of circumstances, until they realize it's a hoax or they're out of funds.

The sharpest difference between the Spanish prisoner scam, the Nigerian letter, and contemporary NFT or crypto rugs, however, is the speed of the con. Fraud's motivation and intended outcome have remained the same for generations—to divorce a victim from as much of their money as possible. The means, however, are accelerated by a new wave of technology. This isn't unique to crypto and NFTs, however. It happens with every innovation renaissance. Web3 is an expedited version of Web2, which was leaps and bounds ahead of Web1. The purpose of technology is to get faster and be more efficient. When used for good and positive reasons, tech makes for better products and happier lives. Conversely, if used for evil, technology harms people and the world faster than ever before.

In the beginning, email enabled quicker communication and reduced paper waste, but bad actors also used the technology to disseminate viruses and wreak havoc on the greater internet. The tech wasn't inherently bad, it's just that there weren't enough guardrails in place to thwart bad actors. The email companies eventually built stronger protection around their services, but it took time. Today, we don't even think twice about logging on. We use email confidently without anxiety of password leaks or security breaches (although they still happen).

We're living in an era of volatile pendulum swings where society and culture are in constant upheaval. This is largely due to the nature of next-gen tech, social media, and algorithmic trends. Mass amounts of people can be moved ideologically with low friction. They can also accumulate and lose wealth in very short periods of time. Blockchain believers are converting at a faster rate than the early dot-com era, but we're also in a mad race to batten down the hatches and board up the windows. As the hurricane descends, the looting is more sophisticated and clever than ever. The fate of NFTs hinges on how fast infrastructure and safety can be integrated into the experience while the creativity flourishes boundlessly.

NFTs are the answer. NFTs are a tool. NFTs are art. NFTs are freedom. NFTs are a scam. At this point in the journey, NFTs can be anything and everything while we collectively determine what we want them to be. But we need *time*. We need to make mistakes, we need distance to gain perspective, and we need to let the space and technology breathe. Until then, it's impossible to cast a permanent definition around NFTs. Whenever someone is proclaimed as an "NFT expert," I say, "An expert on what? We still don't know what NFTs are. And we certainly don't know what they can be or where they're going."

In 1995, *Newsweek* published a piece entitled "Why the Web Won't be Nirvana," in which Clifford Stoll scoffed at the internet for failing on its promises.

"How come my local mall does more business in an afternoon than the entire Internet handles in a month?"

"The truth [is] no online database will replace your daily newspaper, no CD-ROM can take the place of a competent teacher and no computer network will change the way government works."

Stoll kicks off his grievances by noting he's been actively using the web for two whole decades! Today, we see not only how wrong Stoll turned out to be but how nominal twenty years was in terms of technological progression and maturity.

In a follow-up *VICE* interview about his "Line Goes Up" video bashing crypto and NFTs, Dan Olson vents his frustration around crypto's lack of follow-through. Although it's been around for only fourteen years, Olson's of the opinion that crypto never lived up to the hype:

> I've heard all of this before. Venezuela has been on the cusp of switching to Bitcoin for how many

years now? Ethereum has been on the cusp of switching to proof of stake for years, and it never happens. You have to start questioning: Is anybody actually working on those, or are those just hypothetical things that *could* happen?

To Olson, crypto was out of time to prove itself. But just a few months after the interview published, Venezuela replaced its national currency with Bitcoin. That September, Ethereum switched to proof-of-stake consensus after completing the Merge. As it turns out, people were working on fulfilling those promises and they did actually happen. I can't blame Olson, though. These are the advancements with crypto that are often buried under juicier headlines of stupid monkey pictures and million-dollar heists. Dan Olson wasn't wrong. No, not at all. He was just early.

BETTY

Although the NFT narrative is overwhelmed by fast-paced flipping and moneymaking, it's often marketed around the ideals of community and culture. However, there are very few projects that actually do the work. Betty and her husband/cofounder, Psych, started Deadfellaz while raising a family in an Australian beach town. Yet in a short amount of time, they've amassed global fandom, becoming the gold standard when it comes to building a valuable NFT project—not just in terms of floor price, but in terms of inclusivity, supporting artists, and tending to the collectors. Betty has also become a vocal advocate for social and political issues that plague crypto but are often ignored or dismissed. When people ask me what an idealized future of NFTs looks like, I often say, "Betty and the Deadfellaz."

BOBBY: Why is culture important for NFTs to survive?
BETTY: I often compare brand building in the NFT space

to attempting to build something structurally sound on the foundation of a children's ball pit. When you conflate the value of NFTs (and by extension the brand) with the often volatile movements of crypto-currencies, you leave your creation to the mercy of the markets. The pursuit of wealth when things are up will undoubtedly gather people together—but what happens when things inevitably swing downward? There is no substance and nothing to connect with.

Culture is formed over time when people gather around something that holds meaning, incites belonging, or produces an emotional response through shared experience. By building brands around NFTs that have been created with depth and intention—with a clear mission and voice—people can easily connect to that brand on a deeper level. Culture provides a vehicle for social change, a sense of self, belonging, and heart—it isn't quantifiable but provides an anchor of value that is immeasurable and will allow NFTs to flourish despite the turbulence that can be crypto.

BOBBY: Much of the Web3 experience has been narrated in the male voice, with the majority of its participants and notable figures being men. As a woman, tell us the lesser told story that the world should hear. What are the hardships? But also, why do you feel empowered being a woman into NFTs?

BETTY: Web3 currently is centered around the intersections of art, technology, and finance. All those industries are dominated by men—men make up the top 95 percent of traditional fine art sales, they receive over 98 percent of venture capital funding, and they make up the majority of CEO positions in tech. When we look at the intersections of race and gender in those industries, things get even more bleak. As a founder and leader in this industry, I am an anomaly statistically.

Many talk about Web3 as if it is a utopia full of equal opportunity—one where a person can be anonymous and be received for their work first. This is false, in my opinion. The space is being built by the same people who built and work within existing imbalanced structures. The same hurdles to participation exist and will continue to unless true effort is put in by the majority to combat that.

My experience is different from that of my male counterparts in many ways—I would say the hardest one to navigate is online harassment. Successful women with strong voices are not received well in certain online spaces—I receive abuse and threats regularly and have to be careful with things like sharing my location in real time or going to an industry event without security. It's hard. I entered the space anonymously initially—partly to protect myself.

Women in our industry are so often placed in the "women in Web3" box, something that can be used to segregate successful women from successful men—the same way "girlboss" and "She-EO" often do. Panels of women talking to women about being women to an audience of women are often seen, or we are asked to speak only on inclusion rather than on our ideas. This will hopefully change as we continue to challenge things—quicker with men amplifying and showing allyship.

I feel empowered as a woman in this industry because this is the first time I have felt I can have real impact. Everything I do and achieve opens doors for others—the same way there are folks opening doors for me. Women's history, stories, and achievements throughout time have been so often edited or erased. Blockchain technology gives us the power and autonomy to tell our own stories and own them, immutable and forever on-chain. I love being part of that and showing my daughters what is possible.

BOBBY: For many projects to thrive and achieve their goals, their founders are turning to the investment world. Tell us the good and evil that comes with the venture capital conversation. Should Web3 start-ups follow this model?

BETTY: There is no right or wrong way to go about this, in my opinion. I don't think Web3 start-ups necessarily need to raise venture capital to survive or find success. The spirit of Web3 is decentralized and self-sovereign—creators can find support and funding through their community buying their work, earning royalties in perpetuity, and the creation of other revenue streams via brand building, in turn maintaining full control over their creations and trajectories. That being said, often the speed of innovation and developments within the industry require a more stable and sizable chunk of funds outside of crypto. Venture capital does come with benefits such as knowledge, connections, and resources outside of just money. All of these can help with solidifying and scaling—of course, then a certain level of self-determination and independence is lost. Whether that suits a start-up or not is a uniquely case-by-case question.

BOBBY: We met because on the other side of our release, I suddenly found myself feeling very alone. Everyone plays a part in this ecosystem, but for founders, it's an especially turbulent journey. What's it like as a founder in this space? What's the side that nobody sees? And why is it important for us to be there for one another?

BETTY: I remember that day and I will forever be grateful you reached out to me because I also needed a friend like you. Funnily enough, you weren't the first founder to reach out like that. After I launched in August 2021, I quickly found myself often validating and listening to other new founders in my DMs who were struggling after launch.

Founder life is trial by fire, and it isn't something often spoken about for fear of showing weakness. There is an incredible amount of pressure, we're moving at a speed unheard of, and we're hurtling down an untrodden path with no map and all the security issues of colossal companies. We are ultimately responsible for everything we build, while remaining more accessible as leaders and community members than in any other industry I've seen. Unlike Web2 leaders, we are constantly in a stream of feedback—this is an amazing benefit to us because we have the advantage of really understanding our community—but there is also no filter. That, plus the amount of time we dedicate, the speed and the size of it all, can manifest in very unhealthy schedules and declines in mental health.

It is relatively easy to launch an NFT project, but scaling a sustainable brand around that is an entirely different thing that I don't think many are prepared for. I love my job, but I wouldn't be where I am if it wasn't for the support and love from others experiencing the same things, and I'm sure many others will echo that sentiment.

BOBBY: As founders, we quickly became accustomed to FUD (fear, uncertainty, and doubt) from our own communities. Some of it is justified, some of it is hard to hear, and sometimes people are just being outright assholes. How do you stay inspired to build while people are saying hurtful things to your face, complaining about your work, and being cruel?

BETTY: When you create something that comes directly from your heart as creative expression, it becomes really hard to hear negative feedback because it feels so personal. That being said, if you're building a brand or running a project around your creations, it is so important to discern constructive criticism from plain old FUD. When it's especially mean or baseless, I remind myself of my vision and intent—and that people externally don't have the same view of things as we do. They can't see the whole picture. Sometimes the criticism is hard to swallow but fair, which gives us the opportunity to act on suggestions through insights we might not otherwise have had access to. Direct community feedback is a really valuable resource but can be hard to process at times.

I'm a big believer in only creating things you personally feel passionate about or want to see in the world. The passion for my work keeps me inspired in difficult times because the drive to see it flourish comes from a deeper place than just wanting to create a successful brand—I see this as a vehicle for change.

BOBBY: I've seen you do such a great job of onboarding nonbelievers to NFTs. It requires a lot of patience, but even more care. You're genuinely interested in helping artists and creators. How do Web3 and NFTs improve their lives and facilitate their work?

BETTY: I have said before that I'm not in the business of convincing people of anything, and I don't think that is effective—I prefer to lead by example and show people how this space can benefit them through doing those things myself. Having a conversation with someone who is interested and helping them see the opportunities for their specific niche is always fun.

Creative work is typically undervalued—yet creative work is what brings the soul and meaning to almost anything we consume in our world. The value of anything is just a group of people coming together and saying, "Yes, this is worth that much money"—whether it is a tangible item or an idea. In Web3, we've seen NFTs become popular, with art as one of the first contexts—and so the perceived value of art has improved (especially for digital artists).

We've come together and agreed that, yes, art and creativity can be valued in a new way. From a creator's perspective, this presents an opportunity to create art for art's sake in a setting that gets them compensated more fairly for their work—a lack of corporate restrictions, autonomy over where and how it is released, and ownership recorded on-chain.

The way we can easily collaborate in Web3 is also a huge benefit; there are communities forming that amplify one another, support one another, and execute campaigns in a far more effective way than is possible in Web2. We've seen artists mobilize and have massive positive impact in response to causes such as reproductive rights, global conflicts, and protecting the space from becoming predatory and exploitative (artists recently mobilized against a large marketplace that was looking to remove creator royalties).

You're not alone in Web3—you don't have to work in a silo, and you have access to a network of other amazing people all building together.

BOBBY: What's the most common resistance to Web3, and how do you respond to it?

BETTY: Initially, it was the impact on the environment and how the energy it took (gas) for any transaction on-chain wasn't ideal. I've always argued that traditional banking systems use far more energy and have a far worse impact on the environment. Now, of course, following the merge, we have seen carbon emissions from Ethereum reduce by over 90 percent, so the environmental argument no longer stands.

Now I would say the biggest argument is the volatility of cryptocurrency itself, which doesn't acknowledge the culture or community that is formed here, or the potential applications for the technology. I would ask people to look beyond finance. We are building not with the intention of making a lot of money but to change our lives and futures. I want to help shift industries toward more transparent and equitable practices that are people centered. We will see this tech impact most aspects of our lives, so I try to give that context.

BOBBY: Through your collection Deadfellaz, you're always pushing the envelope of what's possible and setting the tone for what's next. In the days to come, how will NFTs evolve? What will Web3 mean and look like in the next few years?

BETTY: I'm very excited for our future here as a collective. Over the last year, we saw many brands formed around NFT projects, and now we're getting to the point where those that launched in 2020 and 2021 are really carving out their niche in their own lane.

I believe we will drop the initialism "NFT" and instead categorize these projects based on their intended utility. We've recently seen "digital collectibles" released by Reddit and being sold by artists through Meta's Instagram. We're moving toward a future where you won't know you're interacting with NFTs at all, and their value will be derived from more than just crypto. I'd prefer people to explore the underlying technology, as I think that provides more personal empowerment and opportunity—and so education is an important focus for us all moving forward.

I believe sentiment is changing from mainstream media and the corporate world toward this space as the brands and tools we create are validated more and more—but I worry that influence will take power from creators who are onboarded that way.

I believe we will see everyone using this technology, from real estate to education to health care.

BOBBY: Tell us what makes Deadfellaz different from the rest of the projects out there. When you explain it to someone, do you call it an NFT brand?

BETTY: Deadfellaz is primarily a proponent of culture. I don't call it an NFT brand because it is so much more than that—it was just born from NFTs. I call it a "brand," but even that doesn't really cover it. It was designed around everything that Psych (my cofounder and husband) and I love. I wanted people to feel a nostalgic, emotional response when interacting with our NFTs, sort of like the feeling of discovering a new band when you're a kid listening to your friend's music.

Our traits are all gender-neutral, and so in the generative process in which those traits were combined with code to produce ten thousand unique characters, none of the resulting characters were inherently gendered. This gives the opportunity for people across the entire spectrum to find themselves within that collection—something that wasn't available when we launched. That inclusivity is something that runs through the roots of what we do as a brand and as a team. We've fostered a safe home for many people who don't feel comfortable engaging with Web3 elsewhere, and this can be seen in a beautiful tangible sense at our events, which are a gorgeous representation of humanity in all its forms.

We're focused on empowering holders with tools to really utilize the IP [intellectual property] of their NFT to form a strong digital identity they truly own.

We have spent so much time and energy presenting ourselves through content we create on platforms that then own that content. We're evolving digital identity and brand building by bridging both Web2 and Web3.

BOBBY: Are NFTs a scam?

BETTY: Haha, if they are, then consider me scammed. No, just kidding. NFTs provide a new opportunity to co-create futures in industries that were closed and rigid and set up to benefit only a certain few. The real scam is the way people are being persuaded by corporations to deny that.

NFTS ARE A
REVOLUTION

After discovering NFTs at the end of 2020, it took me weeks to wrap my brain around the concept. The technical language was dense and off-putting and so much of the logic required blind faith. The one thing that resonated with me, however, was how NFTs could rectify how artists get paid. I wrote this essay shortly after that breakthrough and you can sense the excitement in my voice. It wasn't that long ago, but we were still calling NFTs "cryptomedia" and "cryptoart"— terms that have tapered off with time.

Legendary downtown photographer Ricky Powell died in early 2021, leaving behind a lifetime's worth of hip-hop history gold. Jensen Karp called him "the man who photo'd absolutely everything I've ever thought was cool," much of that attributed to frozen moments in time with rappers like LL Cool J, Beastie Boys, and Run-DMC. Along with Glen E. Friedman, Estevan Oriol, Craig Stecyk, and Chi Modu, my own foray into photography in the nineties was inspired by cultural documentarians like Ricky Powell.

In fact, there was a season when photography led my

career aspirations. I grew up shooting film at concerts and skate sessions, but I most enjoyed taking people's portraits. In the early 2000s, DSLRs and editing programs lowered the barrier of entry to the practice. Smartphone cameras empowered laypeople to be savvy photographers. It became harder to distinguish whether someone was a serious shutterbug or hobbyist. Then, the internet democratized content and social media became a media free-for-all (or a free fall, depending on how you look at it).

Years ago, I shopped my photography portfolio to some select art galleries only to discover that many of them had a policy of not curating photo shows. I then toyed with the idea of producing a photo book but was promptly told by mainstream publishers that photo books are a tough sell.

"Well, what do I do with all these photos I've been shooting since I was twelve years old? Live photos from punk shows and nineties skaters and world travels?"

"Put them where everyone else puts them: Instagram."

I love the medium of photography. Some of my pictures mean more to me than the clothing I design and sell. Yet the marketplace tells me that photos aren't worth as much as physical products because they're easily replicable, drag-and-droppable, and digitally disposable. And it's not just photography. GIFs and JPEGs, memes, captions, MP4s. Whichever the file extension, we've grown accustomed to offering our creative output for free. We've been trained to believe that nobody owns anything on the internet. Online media is to be liberally sourced and shared with all. And there is no monetary value in a tweet or a TikTok.

But that's not true. Your social media posts do make

money. It's just that you don't see any of it. Your gorgeous photographs, compelling essays, and motion graphics draw attention to platforms like Facebook and Google, which churn advertising dollars off all those eyeballs. You do all the hard work. They make the money from it. And now that you see it that way, isn't it incredibly unfair?

I have good news. There's been a revolution welling up to reclaim value and ownership in digital art. With what is now coined "cryptomedia," there is finally a way to restore much of the meaning and value that have been lost. And that's through blockchain technology and non-fungible tokens. Or NFTs.

WHAT IS AN NFT?

Do you remember the Art Basel banana? In late 2019, a duct-taped banana sold at the Miami art fair for $120,000. But, of course, bananas rot, so why would anyone pay that much for a perishable installation? What the patron was actually buying wasn't the physical banana itself, but the certificate tied to the fruit. The artist Maurizio Cattelan clarified that the mushy, decomposing banana can always be swapped out. But there's only one certificate, and that's where the value existed.

NFTs are those certificates recorded on the block-chain. If the banana is a metaphor for your cryptoart (a photo you shot, a song you recorded, a meme you passed around), you can now mark it—or mint it—as an NFT. It's now listed on the blockchain and universally recognized by the world that you are the rightful owner of the work.

Which means that you can sell it. It also means you can buy other people's NFTs.

Where does this all go down? Decentralized marketplaces like OpenSea, Nifty Gateway, and Coinbase NFT. How much money are we talking here? Cryptomedia made headlines when Instagram artist Beeple sold twenty of his pieces for $3.5 million. The more sensational story, however, is the thousands of everyday artists who are striking overnight success and gaining notoriety in this digital gold rush. Estimates are that over $8 million of cryptoart changed hands during the month of December.

On Christmas Day, Sean Williams, a former Cartoon Network intern, accidentally kicked a hole in his wall. As an experiment, he placed a frame around the gash, snapped a photo of it, and minted it on the SuperRare platform. One week later, on New Year's, Sean accepted an offer of 7 ETH for his cryptoart, entitled *Idiot*. As of this writing, 7 ETH converts to roughly $11,000.

WHO IS BUYING THIS STUFF?

I love this question, because it's one that I've been personally hearing my entire career:

"Why would anyone spend three hundred dollars on some basketball sneakers?"

"Five hundred dollars for denim with holes in it? What's wrong with some fifty-dollar Levi's?"

"Who is paying thousands of dollars for a T-shirt? Just because there's a red box on it?"

There's a lot of money floating around out there, especially these days with stimulus checks and stonk surges. And there's a market for everything. We can compare an $11,000 Amir Fallah painting to $11,000 "What the Dunks" or a fancy $11,000 Napa dinner with Screaming Eagle wine. It's relative. One or none of these items may mean as much to you as Sean's photo, but there are consumers out there who will readily justify each expense down to the penny.

Granted, gambling speculators are stirring much of the frenzied activity around cryptoart right now. These are the same types of people who bet big when Bitcoin first broke or squatted on domain names or hedged their investments on real estate in the 2000s. They believe that cryptoart may very well be the next big thing for the internet. And although $11,000 is a lot of money for a digital photograph of a hole, it pales compared to the upside of millions if this is the next Banksy, or billions if it's the next *Mona Lisa.*

I STILL DON'T GET IT. WHY WOULD YOU WANT TO OWN A DIGITAL PIECE OF MEDIA IF IT CAN BE DOWNLOADED ONTO ANYONE ELSE'S COMPUTER? WOULDN'T YOU PREFER A PHYSICAL POSSESSION (E.G., A ONE-OF-ONE OIL PAINTING) INSTEAD, TO ENSURE—AND BRAG TO YOUR FRIENDS—THAT IT'S THE ORIGINAL?

Speaking of Christmas, at the crack of dawn, my boys tore through their meticulously wrapped presents under the tree. Santa gifted them board games, action figures, books, and remote-controlled robots. However, to our dismay, they spent about thirty-five minutes playing with their new toys before diving back into *Fortnite*. For many children today, their realities and social scenes exist within the digital framework of video games. What does it matter if you have a Baby Yoda doll or new Jordans if you can't flex them to your peers in the gaming universe? It's more important to stack digital assets inside the games instead, like back-bling or spray. I could literally hand my kids a hundred-dollar bill and they wouldn't know what to do with it. Instead, they'd ask, "Daddy, can you convert that to *Fortnite* V-Bucks?"

As bizarre and disheartening as this sounds for the kids, you're no different. You spend more time digitally interacting with your friends than seeing them in person. You'd rather curate your page instead of decorating your home. You can hang a painting in your living room for your twenty-five guests a year. Or, you can take a photo of the painting and post it to your social media where thousands of followers will appreciate it.

You can even rotate cryptoart through a digital picture frame: a sunset photograph, Trump's "covfefe" tweet, a Beeple IG video, an NBA Top Shot digital basketball card. Although each slide is a Google Images click away, you can take pride that you own the unique certificate to each of these masterpieces. And that somebody, somewhere, is willing to buy it from you.

SO, WHY ARE YOU SO EXCITED ABOUT THIS?

I'm still figuring this out. Cryptoart and NFTs are so new that history is being made every hour of every day. Most of the insightful editorials, podcasts, and YouTube think pieces on the subject have been recorded in the last month or so.

I think what inspires me the most is that creators will finally be able to make the money they deserve from their hard work. Facebook is a half-a-trillion-dollar company, while many young artists are struggling to make rent. Although the financial rewards aren't the only things that matter in making art, money and compensation help to provide a safe and secure environment to create. And it cuts the lie that your art doesn't hold value or that nobody cares to pay for your work. They do. The market is there. It's just that instead of paying you, the clientele's been paying the social media companies with their time and attention.

Every ten years or so, there's a paradigm shift with the internet. First, it was the transition from portal sites to Google. In the 2010s, social networks flipped not only how we interacted with each other but how we consumed content. Could cryptomedia and NFTs indicate the next wave of how we consider and use the internet? One where everyone, not just artists, stands to benefit as far as property ownership and profitability are concerned?

That shit is bananas.

NFTS ARE FASHION

With the rise of NFTs in 2021, believers started imagining how else blockchain ownership could be employed across different applications. The Metaverse has been a fringe internet dream for decades (think *Second Life*, *The Sims*, virtual reality), but the notion of owning goods that could be interoperable (owned, sold, and used between competing social platforms and video games) reopened the conversation. Fashion is a $3 trillion industry and with more young people interested in their dress than ever, it only makes sense that digital wearables and metaverse clothing have become one of the hottest Web3 sectors to inhabit.

Whenever people talk about metaverse fashion, for some reason, they mention a dress made of fire. "Imagine a dress, but . . . made of fire!" a drunk friend roars, two steps away from minting his idea on the blockchain for a million dollars. It's been a decade since *The Hunger Games*. Is this nostalgic residue from Jennifer Lawrence's twirl on-screen? Metaverse fashion is often portrayed very literally as digital translations of physical garments: a 3D-rendered sneaker or an animated coat. This gown ablaze seems to touch the outer limits of what digital clothing can be. Yet every time I think of Katniss Everdeen on the crypto catwalk, I wonder, why can't she just be the fire?

Metaverse fashion is, like, sooo hot right now. Decentraland is hosting the first Metaverse Fashion Week with Dolce & Gabbana participating in virtual runway shows. Digital fashion designers like Daniella Loftus and stores like The Dematerialised are drawing more customers. In fact, high fashion has been one of the first industries to boldly embrace Web3. Ralph Lauren sold virtual clothes on Zepeto and *Roblox*. Gucci dressed Superplastic characters Janky and Guggimon. Balenciaga delivered *Fortnite* skins and hoodies. Speaking of which, the gaming industry has led the charge. Ten years ago, Diesel introduced their wares to *The Sims*, and prepandemic, Louis Vuitton designed skins for *League of Legends*. There are almost three billion gamers in the world, and it's estimated about 80 percent of them are engaging with digital cosmetics in some capacity.

Even Mark Zuckerberg led his Meta campaign with metaverse fashion. "There is going to be a big market around people designing digital clothing," the Facebook founder declared on the *Lex Fridman Podcast*. That's right. The Zuck is vying to be the most powerful fashion voice on the planet. But then he goes on to envisage how we dress a dragon avatar, which is tickling at best and uninspired at worst. Is this all that awaits fashion in the Metaverse? Garments that burn? Dragons in turtlenecks?

To peer into the future of metaverse fashion, let's first appreciate their respective histories (both the Metaverse and fashion). The Metaverse, for starters, stands for more than an animated environment out of a Facebook commercial. It's also already here and around us, considering how much of our worldviews are cast—and thoughts are distracted—by the internet. Although many equate Web3 to pressing the reset button on the internet, technology is an evolution, building atop and error-correcting its advances. The Metaverse is the next iteration—if not a rebranding—of VR/AR (virtual reality and augmented reality), video games, Zooms and FaceTimes. The word itself was coined by the author Neal Stephenson in his 1992 novel *Snow Crash*. The sentiment, however, reaches further back, long before Ernest Cline's *Ready Player One* or *The Matrix*. The Metaverse is merely our mind and its offerings: dreams, creative ideas, fantasy. It's just that we're now at a point in history where modern technology can add flesh and tissue to these mental objects.

Technology is also to be credited for fashion's genesis. In the fourteenth century, tailoring loose-fitting robes closer to the body amplified personality and human expression. Genders were delineated, clothing was more agile in combat, the abundance of material signified wealth. "Modern fashion emerged when economic mobility gave more people the resources and ambition to express themselves through their attire and new technologies allowed for dramatic advances in the design of garments," writes Richard Thompson Ford in *Dress Codes*. In fact, Ford remarks that this shift in consciousness inspired the "modern individual."

When you combine the two, "metaverse" and "fashion," you're talking about infinite design for boundless self-expression. You can see why I'm so excited about it. For the first time in centuries, fashion is on the verge of redefinition, no longer captive to the laws of physics, earthly materials, social attitudes, and customs. And once again, it's technology (metaverse environments, NFTs, dynamic 3D design) that is unlocking this new way of thinking about what fashion is and what it could be.

Metaverse fashion is as new as the Metaverse itself (so, not that new). In the mid-2000s, *Second Life*, a platform in which residents interact with online environments through avatars, gained in popularity. (*Second Life* is essentially a video game where you don't compete, but socialize.) At the time, L.A.-based American Apparel was a major fashion brand, and so it was splashy news when they opened a shoppable store in *Second Life*. With the click of a mouse, the user could purchase a digital wearable or order its physical counterpart with a quasi-cryptocurrency called Linden dollars. The promise was high, and the hope was even loftier. The shop's designer predicted that by 2007 virtual fashion on *Second Life* would be prolific so long as the developers could build better infrastructure and reduce the friction of mainstream adoption. (Sound familiar?)

Fast forward to this past December, when we rolled out The Hundreds digital wearables on Decentraland, one of the many metaverses. We designed T-shirts, hoodies, caps to be bought and worn by your online avatars at simulated parties. While the NFT community celebrated the offerings, my Instagram followers weren't shy in publishing their disdain.

"This isn't anything new! And the graphics suck!"

Aesthetically, they weren't wrong. Although the revolutionary part was that the metaverse fashion pieces were minted as NFTs on the blockchain (and could therefore be traded as assets on an outside marketplace), the visuals weren't unprecedented or extraordinary. Even I'm baffled by the lack of design progress, and my disappointment goes beyond the medium's graphic format. How is it that fashion in the Metaverse is still trapped in the mentality that it's supposed to mirror physical clothing? The reason for this may exist in the name *"Second Life"* itself. The program was intended to support, if not shadow, our daily existence outside the monitors. This made more sense in the 2000s as people were engaging with the web and social media for the first time. In 2022, however, Americans are averaging forty hours a week online, as much as a full-time job. The rest of the time, our thoughts are being governed by what's happening on the internet, our friendships are maintained through online communication, and there's that nagging Slack DM that needs to be attended to. Many of you may be able to sympathize that the internet is our primary life now.

I mean, look at the youth. In a chicken-and-egg scenario, it's hard to tell which one came first: Kardashian-style contouring or face filters. They're both stuck in a feedback loop. Yet social media influencers have optimized Facetuning and Photoshopping to the point where makeup appears over-the-top in person to translate naturally on-screen. Another example—if you've ever watched a teenager Snapchat goofy facial expressions to their friends, they're mimicking emojis, whereas it used to be the other way around. It also used to be awkward, if not embarrassing, for people to perform for their camera phones in public. The selfie stick, coffee-shop livestreams, and then TikTok dances were markers whereby humans sacrificed physical-world dignity for online clout. Anyone who's done it for the 'gram has treated the Metaverse as their first life and the outside world as their secondary life. Consider the social posturing, virtue signaling, and other methods we employ to communicate our values to social media followers. These are investments into our personal brands in the digital space.

Metaverse fashion, therefore, should be conceived and gestated behind the screen first. (Just from a logistics standpoint, the designer is unfettered by the shackles that slow down the production process. There's not a fashion designer or business today that isn't afflicted with supply-chain issues.) The obvious reason is the capacity to create with abandon. The Metaverse is limitless and so is the designer's artistic latitude. Their digital work then trickles down to the street, instead of the reverse. Just like how Instagram filters influence the way a teenager wears their makeup to school, metaverse fashion will shape what physical fashion looks like on the runways. As silhouettes grow more exaggerated in Sandbox and incorporate otherworldly materials, testing the limits of space and construction, the consumer will shop milder takedown designs in retail stores. Your party dress can't literally be on fire, but its panels can resemble the florid leaves of the flames. And instead of looking costume-ish, your fellow partygoers will be acclimated to the avant-garde design, having seen the original piece prevail in the metaverse marketplace. An old-world illustration of this dynamic is the concept vehicle at a car show. It's an exercise in freethinking art and helps the market visualize where the company is going. Years later, a derivative echo of that model, which carries the same spirit, winds up on the showroom floor.

But we're falling back into the fire-dress way of thinking again, so let's continue the path of drawing different inspiration, or drawing inspiration differently. Instead of mirroring or pulling from conventional notions of physical design, we should look instead to the soul of fashion: quite literally, the soul itself.

The first Zoom was a party. Without context, I messaged the link to some friends, and slowly, confused faces started popping into the room. "Yooo, this is crazy!" The grid reminded me of *Hollywood Squares* or the *Brady Bunch* opener, eyes scanning the boxes to see who else was taking part in the "future." It was noisy. We kept reminding people to mute or unmute and it'd be weeks before we discovered the airbrush filter or how to allow someone to share their screen. But in the first month of pandemic lockdown, many of us transitioned clumsily to virtual meetings and classrooms. Two years later, it's hard to imagine a world where we don't interact through video-conferencing regularly.

I opted for white, uncluttered backgrounds for my

Zoom calls. But then people started facing their cameras toward their bookshelves to appear well-read. Others dropped a colorful painting behind their heads to associate with culture. My friend Chris broadcasted from his sneaker closet, the shelves lined with coveted Nikes and Adidas. Meanwhile, my corner was decked with *Garfield* paraphernalia and band posters.

Confined to our bedrooms during quarantine, we were still looking for ways to express our individuality and stand out on the screen. Most of us didn't stray far from home, so direct-to-consumer sweatpants proliferated. To compensate for—or mask—our slovenliness, the virtual presentation of self became critical. Straightening the picture frames was just as important as the brim on a cap. Nobody could see my rare shoes, so the Zoom "set" was a louder fashion statement.

In "Fashion in the Face of Postmodernity," Charlotta Kratz and Bo Reimer write, "Fashion is more than clothing. Fashion . . . can include items that have nothing at all to do with clothes, items such as furniture, bicycles, skateboards, or even pets." Fashion is beyond fabric and buttons in this way. It's the "cultural construction of the embodied identity."

At this point, we are divorcing the sociology of fashion ("a model of imagined origin [that] follows . . . its actualization through a series of real garments") from semiology.

"Semiology . . . describes a garment which from beginning to end remains imaginary, or . . . purely intellective; it leads us to recognize not practices but images. The sociology of Fashion is entirely directed toward real clothing; the semiology of Fashion is directed toward a set of collective representations . . . The function of the description of Fashion is not only to propose a model which is a copy of reality but also and especially to circulate Fashion broadly as a *meaning*" (Barthes, *The Fashion System*).

Circling back to the Metaverse, if fashion is no longer tied to physical utility (like insulation from exposure) or constrained by gravity or laws of indecency, if its sociological function defers to its semiological definition, what can it now become? The answer lies not in the future, but in the past: fashion's innate function of self-expression. In a *Vogue Australia* piece on digital clothing, The Fabricant's Michaela Larosse states, "Fashion is an emotional experience, and you don't need physicality for that." Fashion's next evolution will begin from the position that if fashion is fundamentally about identity, social status, and signaling, then the Metaverse is a lush, bountiful garden to play in. Because of its liberation from historical precedent and existing systems, the Metaverse will reformat how we consider and engage with fashion.

This is why profile-picture NFTs make so much sense as identifiers. They speak volumes about the tribes we adhere to and the art we admire, especially if one chooses anonymity in the space. PFPs can signal political stances. A World of Women NFT communicates your support for female empowerment, your membership to the Yuga Labs clubhouse, or your level of crypto sophistication. It can also simply mean you support artists. NFTs are fashion in the way my Zoom background is fashion, like the posters on my wall are fashion. It's why I believe that to dress ten thousand generated figures in cartoon clothing isn't the best use case for metaverse fashion. It's redundant, like a hat on a hat. No, the NFTs themselves are fashion. In *Snow Crash*, Stephenson writes, "When white-trash high school girls are going on a date in the Metaverse, they invariably run down to the computer-games section of the local Wal-Mart and buy a copy of Brandy." They aren't shopping at the mall to dress Brandy in virtual denim that simulates the jeans in their dresser. The avatar (Brandy) is the fashion item, a representation of identity, a portrayal of what's socially significant and emotionally resonant to them.

It's fascinating that in a time when people are struggling to key in on identity and purpose, politically homeless and losing meaning in career and church . . . when young people are so uncomfortable in their human bodies to eschew gender categories . . . that the Metaverse enters. Hundreds of years ago, the technology of tailoring instituted identity by conforming fabric closer to one's body. With regards to the wearer, Ford remarks that this innovation "may have helped to shape them by conditioning people to think of themselves first and foremost as unique individuals." Over the centuries, it appears that the clothes became even more expressive as they became more formfitting. Even in the eighties, Donna Karan and Azzedine Alaïa dresses exemplified how "women's bodies were now shaping the clothes, rather than clothes shaping the body" (Hennessy, *Fashion: The Ultimate Book of Fashion and Style*).

Within the Metaverse, the clothing has become so measured and tailored to the body that it becomes one and the same. NFTs are the ultimate vehicle of expression, indistinguishable from the internet self. On the flip side, in the physical world, T-shirt graphics are fashion. If a graphic image is not worn on the body, but draped on a hanger, does it lose its meaning? Of course not. Subsequently, if the graphic is an NFT on a phone, does it not speak for the individual? What if they are holding the phone closer to their body? What if their apparel can broadcast the image like the LED masks that you see at concerts? Funny how as people are breaking out of constraints and classifications design is feeling the same, anxious to discard centuries-old methodologies and patterns of thought.

A decade ago, I was sitting at a conference where buzzwords like "authenticity" dominated the cocktail conversations. The theme of the weekend hovered around VR/AR and how these technologies would radically transform the world. Around the same time, Joaquin Phoenix starred in the sci-fi romance *Her* and one of the things I loved about the film was how Spike Jonze conceptualized an immersive video game environment for Phoenix's character to play in. Fast forward to 2022 and we're not necessarily much further along in realizing these aspirations. Although VCs invested $10 billion in virtual-world start-ups in 2021 (notwithstanding budgets from Big Tech), most people still aren't spending much time in VR/AR. Oculus made for a hot Christmas gift, but Mark Zuckerberg says it will be five to ten years before Meta goes mainstream. Yuga Labs (the team behind Bored Apes) just raised $450 million to build their metaverse but have yet to publish a timeline on when we'll see it. We're in the very nascent stages of metaverse development, a colossal scheme that will require complete overhauls of broadband networks to keep up with the bandwidth, complex agreements between metaverse companies to be interoperable, and the developers to build this field of dreams.

Until then (if it ever actually happens), mass metaverse adoption will continue looking like the Web2, *Roblox*, and gaming worlds we've known for the past ten years. And the first step toward making the virtual our reality will entail settling on a shared understanding. Everyone operates on their own metaverse definition. Mine goes something like this:

If the internet is our Primary Life and Second Life is what transpires in the physical world, the Metaverse is a comprehensive and holistic experience where we don't discern boundaries between both realities.

While we wait for the Metaverse to materialize, much of the sensory gap will have to be filled with our imagination, faith, and suspension of disbelief. We already do that now, translating fonts into our friends' faces as we chat with them. The QR code menu is an apparition of the sticky laminated foldouts at the diner. As I type this, I envision the audience sitting across from me. One day, I'll be able to read your real-time reactions in a virtual theater. Until then, I'll meet your simulated thumbs-up halfway in the meadow of make-believe.

With our brand, The Hundreds, and our NFT collection, Adam Bomb Squad, we've interpreted the modern-day Metaverse as social networks like Twitter and Discord. Although the platforms are Web2 in origin, the conversations and rumination are Web3 in mindset and matter. The communities are organizing as fellowships, not followings. Therefore, The Hundreds has been intentionally dressing as much of the NFT community for the past year to blanket the Metaverse timelines. From the official CryptoPunks purple cap to the BAYC collab in the summer, the Deadfellaz hoodies to our own Adam Bomb Collection of umbrellas, skateboard decks, and plush toys, The Hundreds strives to be the most prominent fashion label in the Metaverse.

Once again, the Metaverse is a comprehensive and holistic experience where we don't discern boundaries between both realities. And so, the best metaverse fashion brands will also lead in the physical spaces. When I speak with luxury housing and clothing companies that are partitioning off standalone Web3 departments, I feel they're missing the point. Web3 is not a clean departure from Web2, it's a maturation. You can't have Web3 without Web2, like you can't disentangle your childhood experiences from your ripened wisdom. At The Hundreds, both departments (fashion and NFTs) are indivisible, each informing the other, in pursuit of the higher purpose: to dress our community in person, online, and within the imagination between. That could mean wearables or PFPs. It could be avatars or streetwear. It can be whatever you want it to be.

And whatever you want to be.

GARY VEE

If there was ever a face of NFTs, it's probably Gary Vayner-chuk. The serial entrepreneur, business influencer, and motivational speaker was one of the first to grab NFTs in a headlock in early 2021 and owned his place in history. Gary was the one who introduced me to CryptoPunks. One night, I was sitting down for dinner with my family when Gary texted me an urgent Zoom link. I was soon sitting on the grid with characters like Logan Paul, Mr. Beast, and Casey Neistat. Gary demanded that we all buy Punks at that moment. It's that type of zeal and belief that not only inspired his own collection, VeeFriends, but also our own Adam Bomb Squad. Once a year, Gary also hosts VeeCon, a stadium-sized expo and festival dedicated to Web3. I can't think of anyone who has more conviction in NFTs. No matter what happens, it's safe to say that Gary's in this to win this.

BOBBY: Much of the Gary Vee story has to do with sports cards. What distinguishes NFTs from other types of collectibles?

GARY: For me, personally, there were a lot of things, but the thing that stood out, number one, was knowing the provenance in perpetuity. I thought that was the neatest thing of all time. How cool would it be for me to know every person that ever owned the Michael Jordan rookie card that I have? So that was what stood out.

Number two: I had just come out of an era where I was very active in the sports card collectible world. And for me, as a very public figure in that world, I didn't like that people were trying to make up things to hurt me and just say that I was pumping and dumping, that I bought all these Zion Williamson cards and I'm flipping them when I never bought a single Zion. And so, I love the transparency of the blockchain. Going through the ups and downs of NFTs in the last eighteen months, one thing that's been great is that people can see that I haven't sold. I am a long-term believer and I like that. So that stood out.

Number three: I liked the idea as a creator and a collector that the originator of the asset could be incentivized on the royalty component. And so that was very different. You know, Marvel doesn't make a dollar after they made Hulk number one, but in this world they would. And I liked that both as a collector and as a creator, obviously.

B: What do you think about the debate around zero percent creator royalties?

G: Here's how I think about it for me: No question, one of the most interesting things about NFTs as a creator is the royalty component. But ultimately, I think that it will ebb and flow. And what I mean by that is that if the royalty component's out, then the creators are not incentivized to continue to add value to the NFT because they won't be able to afford to. I think it's a game of cat and mouse, a game of the seesaw going both ways. If the market overwhelmingly goes to zero, the entrepreneurs that run the projects will have to adjust, thus changing the narrative to the holders. So honestly, I'm not overthinking it because the market is the market is the market, and I'm comfortable with however it goes. If I have to do a series every year to generate revenue, then I can.

B: That's kind of my take on it too. I think it'll be like every other collectibles company where you have editions. There are like one hundred Pokémon sets, and there's, you know, Topps. You do different series every year and you do more mints. I think that's what's best for collectibles.

G: This is where, as a collector, I want the royalties to stay. But as a creator, I'm agnostic. If everybody pushes royalties to zero, I'll just make a new edition every year. And not add anything ever. As a collector, that means the original stuff is going to get trounced.

B: That's true. And I think the creator royalty holds them accountable. Creators are making money off the secondary markets, so we're holding the creators accountable to continue to provide utility.

G: I don't think it's an accountability. I think it's aligned interests.

B: Obviously, CryptoPunks, you were just really early on it. You're the one who put me on to it. So what was it that you saw and you knew that a lot of people just didn't get at that time? I'm just trying to go through your mindset. I'm assuming this is end of 2020 . . .

G: This was the end of 2020, and what I understood was that I already thought that NFTs could happen in 2017 with CryptoKitties. I mean, that was like a five-minute thought. I didn't even buy one. But I thought, "This hypothesis could work. Let me keep an eye on it and see if it hits a critical scale." Then in 2020, I'm like, "Wait a minute, this could happen. Oh, wait a minute, Punks is the one." And Punks is the one because then all these other ten thousand collection things are popping up and they're following the Punks model. So, then history is on the side of Punks. And I start doing a lot of homework and spending time on Discord and studying ERC 721. And I'm like, "Okay, this is the fucking one."

So now my brain goes into VeeFriends. My brain's going into my contemporaries, my head's going into, "I'm going to do something." My contemporaries who are creative, they're going to do something, and all this is going to happen and it's all going to beckon back to Punks. Me and Bobby and Apes and World of Women and Doodles and all of us—we're going to have to actually execute. For Bored Ape to work out, it actually has to become Nike. It has to be evergreen, iconic for a long time. It can't be Z. Cavaricci. It can't be Lacoste. It can't be Guess. It can't be Lee. It has to run the gamut. Same with VeeFriends. Same with you. Same with everything.

B: That's hard to sustain.

G: Apes can do it if they are as good as Nike. Reebok and Adidas have had their moments, right? But Nike has actually done it. And so, you know, for me, that's what I'm trying to do with VeeFriends. Can I be Nike? Can I, for thirty, forty, fifty years, sustain cultural relevance, demand interest, intrigue, character development?

B: Speaking of VeeFriends—there's a distinction between the traditional, typical collections and the blue chips in the NFT space, like VeeFriends. What makes the difference if someone is building a collection today? What should they be doing? How should they be thinking?

G: The operator, long term, actually being able to make people care. In the short term, these were the best projects of a moment in time. I'll give you an example. The Clash was the best punk band in this little five-year window that captured the imagination. And they've been able to ride on that for forty years. To me, the verdict is still out on all of us. VeeFriends included. At the end of the day, I think that it's all going to come down to execution.

B: You always say 99 percent of these projects are going to fail. How do you end up in that winning 1 percent?

G: Same. Execution. You just look back at intellectual property. GI Joe dominated in the sixties, died in the seventies, came back in the eighties, right? Transformers crushed the mideighties, died for fifteen years, came back in the early 2000s. It's just execution.

B: You said from the beginning, Guys, I'm putting

everything on the line by doing NFTs—my business, my reputation, my career.

G: I think that's what I was looking at. Who else do you know who is going to do that? And I mean, look, if the economy gets ripped here, I'm going to really pay attention to and buy up a bunch of stuff from the people that give me a sense that they're really trying to do this for another fifteen years.

B: Speaking of the next fifteen years and the future, what does it look like to you with NFTs? Do we still call them NFTs? Is it still the way that we do these collectibles?

G: I think they'll be a small percentage of collectability energy, because that's how the world works. There are a lot more people using tickets to go to events and using black cards to buy things. And that's bigger than people collecting art sneakers and sports cards. But art, stickers, and sports cards are still a massive category. There'll be plenty of collected NFTs, but they'll be smaller. The 2021 hysteria made people think all NFTs were worth $10,000. I was yelling at the top of my lungs that that was actually not going to be true at all.

B: Okay, last question: What do you say when someone says NFTs are a scam? Are they a scam?

G: I don't react to it. I say that they may be right. But I completely disagree. And that in 2037, this will be solved and the debate will be ended. And somebody is going to be right.

B: And it's going to be . . . Gary!

G: When people say NFTs are a scam, they're saying

Beanie Babies were a fad. What they don't understand is that they may be right about an individual project. When I hear somebody saying NFTs are going to be a fad, I think, "You don't understand." Stuffed animals are going to be here forever. I don't know if it's Beanie Babies or Raggedy Ann or Care Bears. We're looking at it on the macro scale. They're looking at it from the perspective of "I don't think Bored Apes or VeeFriends is going to be worth anything." They may be right. But something's going to replace that energy in that macro technology.

B: That's exactly what it is.

G: They're saying Beanie Babies are going to be worth nothing. And I'm saying, "You're right. I agree." I'm saying 99 percent is zero, but stuffed animals are forever. And NFTs are forever; what fills them will ebb and flow. And I'm hoping that VeeFriends is one of them forever. I'm hoping VeeFriends is the teddy bear.

NFTS ARE
STREETWEAR

It was impossible not to draw comparisons and parallels between streetwear and NFTs early on. Having spent the last two decades of my life immersed in streetwear, it was apparent that much of NFTs' collectability and mechanics were derived from the very culture we helped formulate. Since this essay, NFTs have been able to transcend the bounds of streetwear methodology and in some ways pick up where streetwear left off. This is due to the speed and Herculean power of the technology as well as a new economics and gamification of the product.

It's impossible to define a point in time when "streetwear" was born. No matter where you begin the streetwear story, you start in the middle. There was always an act of resistance that preceded it, an artistic defiance of a system. "Streetwear" is also understood as different things to different people by generation and geography. It can be the New York hip-hop brands of the eighties; it might mean Stüssy beach culture or Diamond skate luxury. Streetwear can be Nike or secondhand shops like Round Two. I've even seen athleisure brands co-opt the title. But the larger mainstream now classifies streetwear as casual sportswear/workwear aligned with a scarcity mindset, elitist attitude, and "hype" marketing vis-à-vis Veblen goods. Much of the appeal comes by way of heightened social status. Streetwear is a subcultural badge, a cool-guy co-sign, a blue-check on a lapel.

For the last decade, streetwear brands—most notably New York–based Supreme—set the tone for how a brand could stay culturally relevant, artistic, and innovative, and still be a capitalist machine. The frenzied lineups, the collaborations, and the celebrity endorsements galvanized an entire generation of entrepreneurs to be the Supremes of their own industry, whether it was fashion or food or farming. Business start-ups that were motivated not only by money but by Cool and Clout, took pages out of the streetwear book: make the product in limited editions, do "drops" that immediately sell out to rouse froth and FOMO, and play into the resale market (without acknowledging it exists). Of course, streetwear learned much of this from high-fashion and niche collectibles, but its twist was that it made it "cool," youthful, and accessible on a street level. Like rap music, pop culture glommed on to streetwear, and now, social hierarchy isn't defined solely by money or class, but by access to the underground and the validation of teenaged gatekeepers.*

---

* This probably has a lot to do with how social media corralled us all into the same room when it comes to the right music to listen to, the most up-to-date slang, and the right brands to endorse. Can you think of any other time in history when grown adults cared so much about keeping pace with teenagers?

In fact, crypto might be one of the most significant cultural trends of the last ten years that isn't influenced by adolescents at all. NFTs appear to be of little interest to many teenagers.* The stocks/trading features might be out of bounds, if not unappetizing (most young people live for the moment and aren't champing at the bit to invest). The collectibles side of it can be appreciated only by people who are old enough to be nostalgic about hoarding something. But there is the art and status element that has tractor-beamed a younger generation in. And so, it only follows that they'll desire—if not expect—their favorite streetwear brands to follow.

The longer I play in crypto, the harder it is to ignore NFTs' parallels with—if not direct inspiration from—streetwear on both the design and social fronts. Scott Sasso, pioneering founder of 10.Deep, agrees. "It all looks and feels like 2005, 2006 streetwear. All these start-ups of dorky, cartoon-themed PFPs and building a community around those things." As a status symbol, NFTs are metaverse fashion identifiers. OG sneakerhead Franalations says, "Early on, camping out and stuff, you'd see this box logo or this Neighborhood collab and that to me was a badge, showing you were there, at that place at that time, you knew about that release then. And that's pretty much what NFTs are designed to do and show." Steven Vasilev, cofounder of NFT and digital fashion brand RTFKT, goes further: "NFTs are bigger than just streetwear. For the past two hundred years, people have been buying

* According to a Piper Sandler report in October 2022, 55 percent of teenagers had heard of NFTs, but only 5 percent had purchased one (87 percent of them being male).

physical items to show their status and now you can have a (Crypto)Punk which is a digital Lamborghini."

Although streetwear (which at this point is arguably an aging institution) can learn much from the decentralization and technological capabilities afforded by NFTs, this essay is to suggest that NFTs can learn from the success and travails that streetwear has experienced along its journey. The overarching message is that culture and community must outweigh the transactional aspects of the game. Although quick flips and trading are essential to collectibles culture, they cannot become the only thing that drives a project. Once that happens—and there are signals that this is already a rampant attitude in the NFT space—the players will move on to the next fix or gadget. Sneakers, art, watches, BMWs, and vintage T-shirts, I get it. In 2021, everyone is now an investor. But do we want all things fun, creative, and tradable to feel like and emote as stocks? In their current iteration, NFTs can hold the world's attention only for so long before they're distracted by the new shiny object. That is, unless the NFT is grounded in something irreplicable and irreplaceable. Long-standing rewards and enduring benefits that are human and meaningful. Much more than a generic financial gain.

One of my concerns (of a few!) with NFTs is that even before they've gone mainstream many newcomers are already looking to them as investment pieces first and art pieces and cultural artifacts second (community membership third?). When thousands of ordinary people are becoming overnight millionaires by selling cartoon JPEGs, spun through the amplification and acceleration of social media, it's no surprise that the dollar signs in eyeballs obstruct the deeper intent and purpose of blockchain art.

Streetwear, conversely, had a good decade of runway to build the artistic appreciation and cultural foundation before reselling stole the narrative. In the late '90s and early 2000s, a sneaker message board called NikeTalk was the precursor to the crypto Discords of today. (The difference would now be that every NikeTalk member can set up their own NikeTalks for their personalized audiences. This is as overwhelming as it sounds!) Although flipping sneakers was an active and vital part of the culture, we didn't have the infrastructure to facilitate the volume of transactions you see now. Craigslist, eBay, and Yahoo! Japan were the only online marketplaces to buy and sell other people's shoes, but most collectors were wary of scams and sharing their identity and credit card information over the internet (sound familiar, NFTers?). NikeTalk, therefore, was a forum to share news on releases at concrete retailers, discuss the art and product design, and socialize with other like-minded collectors. In fact, most of the action took place in the General Forum, which barely touched on the topics of sneakers at all. The rare Nike retros brought the people together, but their real lives intertwined around more mundane conversations. And instead of focusing only on reselling, it was habit for NikeTalk members to don and crease their shoes in the "What Did You Wear Today?" thread. The status came not in the money profited off the item, but in that you were informed about—and could locate and access—the sneakers in the first place. If you had done the homework to find the right retailer, waited in line, and ponied up the retail price for the Nikes, stomping around in SB Dunks or Wovens were as good as a fancy PFP today.

Because we had this window of time to lay the roots of sneaker culture, even as it's become a billion-dollar industry boosted by resellers and secondary marketplaces like StockX, the shoe game sustains because it is moored to a legitimate history and lore. Even if you never break the box open before you ship shoes out to the next flipper, it's taught that Tinker Hatfield or Hiroshi Fujiwara left their mark on the leather, and that their opinions and repertoire offer meaning to sneakers as art. What happens when the brands fail to tout the value of artist-led design and cultural energy?

At the end of 2021, a Nike internal meeting worried that their core customers were leaving for smaller, independent brands because of a lack of emotional connection. "We're gonna shape the marketplace to reflect the community we serve . . . so that we actually show and we actually give equity and inclusion to the communities that have been gentrified out and alienated by the resale market." Nike acknowledges the critical function of culture in upholding sales and growth. "High heat, hype is 'killing the culture.'" Vasilev of RTFKT emphasizes this point as a driving reason for their NFTs' success: "One of the key points is culture. That's why everything we do, we introduce new artists." In 2021, RTFKT collaborated with NFT wunderkind FEWOCiOUS on a $3 million drop, selling out their virtual sneaker editions at $3,000, $5,000, and $10,000.

Speaking of which, the most glaring void in NFTs is the lack of collaborations. Meanwhile, streetwear understands all too well that collaborations not only fuel hype but lend cohesion to a stable marketplace. The reason being that collaborations build trust. And brand-building is all about cultivating faith with the customers.* Streetwear, in its early days, was devoid of any type of fraternity outside of its neighborhood cells, and so the good secret stayed relatively secret. Okay, fine, streetwear was much cooler before outsiders could access it, let alone learn about it. But once brands reached across the internet to find one another (think The Hundreds meets Mighty Healthy and Married to the Mob over cold emails) and work together, we built a taller stage to perform. Collaborations not only served our wallets, but they bridged our worlds and unified our customers. Most importantly, they dispelled suspicion and forged trust with curious shoppers. "If these two names believe in each other/streetwear, then I believe in them/it too."

NFTs are still in the dark ages, quite figuratively. Crypto anonymity adds a thicker layer of apprehension and anxiety. With higher stakes at play, the FUD (fear, uncertainty, doubt) is very real. Like early streetwear, many NFT collectors and leaders hide behind pseudonyms (on NikeTalk: Dirtylicious, Swoshmn) and most NFT artists and brands are isolated in tribes (one of streetwear's first brands was Tribal from San Diego). The *New York Times* columnist David Brooks defines tribalism as the antithesis of community, and in the case of NFTs, this is accurate if you look at the space between Discords and the

* Brand-building is also about cultivating faith *between* the customers. It's a social contract where everyone miraculously agrees that a made-up brand is, like, an actual, valuable thing now.

gaps within crypto society. That is why many collectors get so excited when celebrities, brands, and even institutions thumbs-up NFTs. These are warm, entrusted, and recognizable faces that say, "It's okay. I'm here in the dark with you." I'm not saying founders need to reveal their identities,* but the NFT world must continue to work on building trust not only with their own communities but between. Collaborations between brands, projects, and designers can be the tissue that binds.

In November 2017, ComplexCon hosted its second annual streetwear convention in Long Beach, California. The year prior, ComplexCon was an undeniable success, inviting thousands of young people from around the world to experience their favorite brands in their environments. But ComplexCon 2 leaned too far into the reselling side of sneakers and streetwear. Instead of a skate ramp or a gallery, eBay was the centerpiece of the arena as a main sponsor. There was more marketing emphasis placed on exclusive Nike shoe drops than on the designers and artists who made them. And as a result, the attendees were motivated by flipping more than participating in—or supporting—the culture of streetwear. Resellers got into fights; booths were shut down over violence. And the following year, ComplexCon corrected back to a more measured balance between transactions, art, and culture. Today, streetwear and sneakers are bigger than ever and ComplexCon continues to be a world's fair for all things street culture.

* It was several years after starting The Hundreds that Ben and I published a photograph of ourselves. Some streetwear designers, like Zac FTP, still hide their faces.

Of all the similarities between NFTs and streetwear, there are just as many differences. One of the biggest being that the cycles and timelines are expedited by technology and crypto's volatile nature. Fashion operates on a hyperactive schedule of hills and valleys, but trends can often subsist for years. Meanwhile, NFTs have survived a couple of market dips just in the last six months alone and the outfacing trends have thrived and died on the vine. As Scott Sasso referenced earlier, sometimes I look around at all these cartoon profile-picture NFT projects and am struck by the memory of streetwear designs in the early 2000s. In that era, every designer and brand followed one another down the path of colorful characters and illustrated graphics. Once the market had its fill, it took only a few settlers to upset the trend by banding together and responding to the status quo with a contrary aesthetic. The next chapter of streetwear went dark and minimal with graphic designs. If there were pictures on T-shirts and hoodies, they were photography-based, typography-driven, and starkly literal. The Americana trend of men's fashion and then streetwear's first turns on the Paris runway expunged the graphics entirely. Fifteen years later, cartoony T-shirts have returned to streetwear but only because the audience has expanded so widely, every style and genre can be accommodated. And now, those Adjective Animals as I like to call them (A Bathing Ape, Pink Dolphin, Rare Panther) have reincarnated as NFT collectibles (Bored Apes, Cool Cats, Pudgy Penguins). It makes sense when you remember that the people designing these also grew up wearing the early streetwear labels.

In my opinion, NFTs in their current aesthetic—not in

their utility or purpose—won't last as the predominant artistic representation of collectibles. I don't exactly know what this means for existing NFTs when these tokens are burned onto the blockchain forever, but I can foresee a next chapter where the visual assets have to adapt and update to match a contemporary trend in the space. Or maybe they will be used to unlock a 2.0. What we do know already is that photography NFTs (see Dave Krugman, John Knopf) are already gaining traction. And that some projects are experimenting with more video and motion. If we've learned anything from NFTs, it's to not be married to the present state and understanding of technology. On October 11, 2021, NFTs are cute Adjective Animal trading cards that are weighed against one another by a third party's rarity ranking score. They offer very little real-world utility or purpose outside of the potential for trading gains, social identity, and access to a community. But on October 12, 2021? That can all be easily disrupted by new settlers, by an artist waiting in the wings with a brave, opposing idea, or a turn in the technology that allows for futures unimagined.

With our project Adam Bomb Squad, we'd rather prepare for maps with no roads than a road map. Streetwear taught us about the power of community and culture. Streetwear revealed the secret of collaborations. But the greatest thing we learned from streetwear—that we are applying to our NFTs—is that nothing lasts forever and tomorrow is uncharted. Trends will rock this market. Ethereum will go in and out. The survivors are the ones who improvise through the droughts. The winners know to adapt to the terrain. And the last brands standing are founded on a rock-solid core, rich with history and relationships. Fashion and NFTs go out of style, but people never do.

"It's still cash-grab season, but cash-grab season is gonna end. And people are gonna have to provide the substance," Scott says in the final minutes of our call. "People think it's all the same thing, but it's not gonna be. And the paths forward are gonna be very different."

NFTS ARE CULTURE

There are so many NFT summits now that I joked, "All of this work is getting in the way of my NFT conferences." Art Basel, NFT LA, VeeCon, Consensus, Metaverse Miami, just to name a few. Not to mention the regional conferences, developer conferences, crypto-specific conferences, and gaming conferences. We don't need this many conventions, but they do serve a purpose for an industry that is assembling so rapidly, online discourse alone isn't efficient enough. When thousands of crypto thought leaders gather in a city's arenas, Michelin-star restaurants, and bars to build the future together, witness the frenetic energy of a delirious Discord but spun with loose alcohol, antsy ETH, and COVID anxiety.

NFT.NYC is held twice a year by an organization nobody can quite tell me anything about. Although the official conference draws thousands of people into the city, many never step foot into the venue. It's like South by Southwest in that way. There's the actual show and then there are the outside events, which for many can be the main attraction.

NFT.NYC has never reached out to us (even though Adam Bomb Squad randomly won an award in 2022), so the past couple of conferences, we've organized our own activations. Last fall, we hosted a live *Bomb Talk* (my Twitter Spaces talk show) and threw a party with Steve Aoki. In 2022, we opened a The Hundreds pop-up shop with NFT-related apparel in SoHo. We staged a fake NFT protest with paid actors that went viral. I conducted another live *Bomb Talk* conversation, this time with Spike Lee. And we threw one of the best shows of the week with Pusha T in Times Square.

It's funny because going into it, most of us were nervous that the sentiment would be low considering the crypto bear market. Perhaps because we were anticipating the worst, it kinda sorta turned out to be the best? This, exclusively from the standpoint of community building, networking, and solidifying relationships. Friendships flourished and only bolstered my confidence in the work. I made so many new friends that it comforted me to know how many smart, capable, and powerful figures are backing the tech.

However, I wouldn't say there was much new noise in the sense of innovation or technical development. Doodles announcing Pharrell as their Chief Brand Officer was splashy, and blue-chip projects like Cool Cats and Azuki had incredibly fun activations. The Bored Apes held their music festival throughout the week with performances by LCD Soundsystem, HAIM, and Eminem. It was mainly vibes.

Meanwhile, there was an incident leading up to NFT.NYC that stayed in the back of my mind as the days unfolded. To generate hype for their Ape Fest, the Bored Ape Yacht Club stenciled their logo around the city in the spirit of guerrilla marketing. Most of the campaign was harmless, sprayed on the pavement with temporary paint. The marketing company that was hired got carried away with one specific placement, however. This employee must've assumed the NEKST bomb on the former Germania Bank wall was neutral grounds. What's wrong with tossing in an ape skull for good measure? After all, the surrounding environment is layered with decades of tags and throw-ups.

Well, for one, they clearly weren't aware of the street politics of going over another tag (which is something you probably should be aware of if you get paid to stage street-art stunts). Second, of all the walls, it wasn't wise to deface one by NEKST, a luminary in the graffiti world whose name has been protected on Bowery and Spring since his passing a decade ago. In fact, when the current owners bought the building for $55 million, they enshrined NEKST's name out of respect not only for the artist but for New York's underground graff community.

It didn't take long for the internet to flame BAYC. First, graffiti Instagram took turns scolding the Apes for their overstep. Within twenty-four hours, the social commentary ran the gamut from trolling dunks to vicious threats. This didn't come as a surprise since BAYC is no stranger to controversy. They are, after all, the biggest target. As the marquis brand in a space that is subject to scorn and public challenge, every wrinkle is examined and exploited, from Discord scams to the gas fees around their land sale.

I can think of a few instances where NFTs have rubbed up awkwardly against deep culture. I remember when the designer Virgil Abloh passed at the end of 2021, a popular NFT voice and BAYC holder made the effort to tweet "I have NO idea who Virgil is" amid people mourning. Short-lived projects break into the space proclaiming their position as the "Supreme of NFTs." Some brands see themselves as high fashion yet refer to their clothing as "merch." As NFT projects and artists race to justify their value, they're hastily slapping on any badges of cultural validity, but the experience is thin and clearly fabricated.

Although going over a NEKST piece warrants outrage, the anger wasn't just about that. It wasn't even really about BAYC. The tension between the graffiti world and the Apes was undergirded by a deeper frustration simmering around NFTs and crypto. Regardless of which side of the line you stand on, I think we can all agree that there is a complacent—and almost impudent—ignorance within segments of the NFT community when it comes to outside culture. In fact, part of this nose-thumbing is what makes NFTs remarkable to begin with. The technology allows neophytes to circumvent the gatekeepers and the tastemakers. Historically "cool" cultures like music, graffiti, streetwear, tattoos, and skateboarding are bound with tradition, hierarchies, and earning respect. One must pay dues, signed off by an order of predecessors. NFTs brush that process aside, granting everyone access and letting the marketplace determine who floats.

This is the reason why NFTs' loudest influencers were relative unknowns twelve months ago. It's why emerging artists and brands perform better than established physical-world artists and companies. Of course, there are social puppeteers who affect trajectories, but for the most part, an NFT's growth is determined by the people, not the media, tastemakers, or other systems. This frustrates those who believe in pecking orders and preserving power, but I absolutely love this about NFTs. It foils all the BS around family trees, industry politics, and blocking.

The canyon between crypto and culture must be traversed, however, if we want NFTs to have credibility and acceptance in the broader marketplace. Cultural awareness will make NFTs more familiar to an outsider and more friendly to a nonbeliever. It's the same reasoning behind celebrity endorsements, a Jimmy Fallon wink, and token-gated concerts headlined by popular musicians. As much as our waking moments are consumed by the digital universe, most of our reality is still tethered to cultures in the physical world. And the more correspondence between the two sides of the looking glass, the further the boundary dissipates. Cultural sensitivity also contributes to the holistic betterment of NFTs. Being attuned to other cultures opens NFTs up to alternative insight, collaborative opportunities, and surprising innovation. As someone who has led hundreds of collabs over the years, I can attest to the population growth that comes with cross-cultural exposure.

Although it is important for the NFT community to be mindful of outside culture, it might be even more critical to develop culture of its own. Think of culture as the rich soil base for the ecosystem. NFTs have made significant progress in reaching across to the mainstream and on-boarding millions of newcomers to the wonders of block-chain ownership. Yet for them to plant deep roots, there must be a hospitable alternative to other cultures and an incentive to chill. For one, we need social rewards like community with shared values and goals.

The anthropologist E. B. Tylor defines "culture" as "that complex whole which includes knowledge, belief, art, morals, law, custom, and any other capabilities and habits acquired by man as a member of society." In *Urban Sustainability in Theory and Practice*, Paul James adds that culture is "a social domain that emphasizes the practices, discourses and material expressions, which, over time, express the continuities and discontinuities of social meaning of a life held in common."

I trace it all the way back to how brands and communities are codified in the first place. In almost every culture and subculture, the origin story begins with a group of people who are drawn to an art, who dedicate themselves to the craft and creation of this interest without any forethought of profitability or scaling. In fact, the most authentic cultures rally in rejection of money. As the phenomenon grows and attracts more devotees, outside corporate hawks take interest, seeing an opportunity to build infrastructure and capitalize off the zealous few. Some cultures—like hardcore, for example—resist this type of growth. Others—like streetwear, perhaps—eventually adopt (or succumb to) the commercial expansion.

NFT brands, on the other hand, do this backward. Largely because of the mechanics of the marketplace and the basic technology in valuing a project's worth (conflating secondary floor price with consumer conviction), the focus from the very start is not on art appreciation but on how much money can be made by selling the product. You can immediately see how antithetical and counterproductive this mentality can be in forging brand loyalty. It also establishes the community on a very feeble foundation. All money is green. In metaverse speak, cash is interoperable. If your primary objective is to get richer, there will always be other avenues to explore: the next crypto, the new NFTs. If you haven't cultivated a connection with the art, the practice, and the rituals, you won't stick around when the profits narrow. (We're seeing this firsthand with the bear market.) You'll migrate to pastures where the money is greener.

So the big question is how do we create an authentic, meaningful culture around NFTs? Is the collective interest of investing and flipping enough to bind a community together? Or do we need to drill deeper than that? And why would a collector want to associate with—or even identify as—a specific NFT brand? Everybody wants to be the Supreme of the space, but do they think about how Supreme curates their own community?

This brings me back to NFT.NYC week. Night after night, I bounced from one party to the next. There was a clear upgrade from the last NFT.NYC, when the standard of a holders' event hovered somewhere between pizza-box frat party and shoestring Comic-Con activation circa 2009. Most every function this time around featured a notable DJ, band, or rapper. The venues were top-shelf thanks to corporate sponsorships. Yet, once again, we were running things in reverse. Parties are spaces to celebrate a culture, not a culture in itself. What exactly were we congregating for?

People want to be a part of something. Remember what James said: "A life held in common." Yes, they want to join a community, but it must be centered around a joint cause or obsession. If it's just about ETH, there's no distinction between the Ether gained by trading one project over another. I've seen this play out in our own project, Adam Bomb Squad, with collectors who profess allegiance to the bombs only to adopt a new avatar as they trade up the ladder. Some of those people will last the shortest amount of time in the space because their avatar isn't a bomb or a zombie or a punk. Spiritually, it's the Ethereum logo and their tribe is currency, which can always be mined more conveniently elsewhere. Money isn't a culture. In fact, it's argued that it's the opposite force. The surrounding behaviors and rituals to get to the money, however, can very well make up a legitimate culture.

Critics decry NFTs as superficial if they only see currency as the culture. I think that's fair. On a cursory glance, most Telegram groups are focused on flips and the media loves a big sale (or steal). But NFTs also espouse agreed-upon principles and worldviews like decentralization and fairness for artists. NFTs follow customary practices like alpha chats, minting drop mechanics, and decentralized autonomous organizations (DAOs). "Culture" has been defined differently throughout history, but in the twentieth century, authors like Dick Hebdige emphasized the code and symbolism around culture as a means to communicate experiences socially. In NFTs, that signaling is performed through social media PFPs and metaverse avatars. Contrary to media coverage, there is also a cultlike appreciation for the art, whether it's the Tezos community or the work of blue-chip NFT figures like ThankYouX, FVCKRENDER, and Amber Vittoria.

And finally, the true test of a culture is its relational bonds. Cultures are often decided by how they differ from other clubhouses, furnishing a sanctuary for the socially displaced and discontented. I find that many in the NFT community have exhausted inspiration in their native sectors or are desperate to resolve a nagging Web2 problem. NFTs are not only a gold rush of crypto but also fresh ideas and pioneering dreams. As sterile as an NFT conference can be, it can be a birthing ground for a movement. Much of modern streetwear's cultural heritage can be attributed to tradeshows like ASR, MAGIC, and Agenda. Skateboarding can say the same for shop demos and corporate contests. Those cultures weren't conceived on the Paris runways or behind the granite counter of a downtown boutique. They were birthed on hungover conversations in the shaded, boring corners of a convention hall. The only obstacle with NFTs is time. While this space is in a hurry to build a culture, there is no expediting an organic forested network of collaborations, conflicts, and milestones. Sometimes you just gotta let it grow.

I had a great time in New York making new memories with a burgeoning community. But as I crisscrossed the Lower East Side hitting NFT events, I kept stumbling into figures I've known for half my life in streetwear. People like Tremaine Emory of Denim Tears, Mike Malbon from Frank's Chop Shop, the tattoo artist Luke Wessman, and Kevin Bailey from Vans. I even had a chance encounter with James Jebbia, the founder of Supreme, around the corner from our former New York flagship. We didn't chat about streetwear much because we'd said all that needed to be said. Instead, we discussed family, global affairs, and summer travels. For a brief window of time, I felt at home, having spent the week roaming the foreign NFT.NYC terrain. I cherish specific memories over the years with each of these individuals, and as streetwear history trudges along, their contributions comprise a golden tapestry of indelible culture. It made me sentimental for the past and also curious about the future. I wondered about the conversations I'll hold with my NFT friends twenty years from now and what we'll see when we look behind us. There is no telling what NFT culture will be, but I'm excited to get started.

In the end, I knew nothing would come of the BAYC NEKST situation. The NFT space has the memory of a goldfish—not just for market trends, but also scandals and tea. By the time Questlove fired up his turntables at Ape Fest, the NEKST wall was a distant memory to most of the NFT community, the only faint reminder being BAYC stencils crossed-out by someone else's aerosol tip across SoHo sidewalks. By now, I'm sure most of those ape skulls have washed off the pavement, the ink sloughing off into the sewer grates with the rest of the city soot. Those black Xs will remain, however. The permanent paint baked deep into the streets of New York City.

MEL TAL

A big reason why I love NFTs is simply because the technology has attracted some of the brightest minds and innovative thinkers from around the world. Of course, many are drawn to the money, but the ones who are making the most impact are driven by helping people and changing the world for the better. This includes my friend Mel Tal, who is the smartest person I know in Web3 and a beacon in the fog of FUD and bad actors. Mel is a secret weapon behind some of Web3's most prominent brands, like Nike, Time, Rug Radio, and Autograph, and she has always been there to help me see the problem differently. When I was thinking of people to interview for this book, her name came first, because listening to her speak about NFTs and crypto can convince even the most resistant doubters. If you're confused or questioning the need for Web3, try looking at it from Mel's point of view...

BOBBY: So we're seeing crypto crash once again, but it's nothing new for those who've been doing it a long time. Is there anything about this current cycle that you would say is different than the others?

MEL: I think the biggest difference is that it's impacting more people. And the bigger the industry gets, the more impact there is when things oscillate, like in these really high highs and low lows. So that impact then spreads out more, and there's more media and more people know about it. And so it matters more, right? Whereas in 2017, a lot happened, probably similar to now, but most people didn't know about it. And most people still don't know about it because it was very insular, and even the media coverage was so low that you can't look back at it and see some big thing—it was very niche. Now, when it's sort of infringing on the retail world and normal everyday people and media and politicians and personalities, all talk about it becomes a much, much bigger thing. That's part of growing up. The industry has to grow up in the way that it shows up—and that's going to be part of the next learning curve.

B: One of the most common accusations with crypto and NFTs is that they're Ponzi schemes. How do you define a Ponzi and do you agree or disagree with the accusations?

M: Well, it's about intent. What's the intention behind doing anything? Let's say you take crypto out of it because there are Ponzis everywhere. Is there a bad intent behind whatever you're putting out? Are you doing this to extract value without giving any in return? The problem that you get inside the crypto space is that it's a lot easier to extract value because the whole notion of the technology is built around value and moving value in an ecosystem. So then you see these very extreme expressions of value, and the Ponzis seem more crazy than what you see elsewhere.

But no, I don't think it's a Ponzi. I think that people will come and use this technology like every other technology that's ever come before it. It can be a Ponzi. But also, people will come and use it in a way that will change systems for the better. It's just a choice. And it's about us then saying, "Okay, well, how do we as individuals decipher and make better choices of the things that we choose, so that the Ponzis don't get our attention and the things that have legitimacy do?"

B: Decentralization is a core tenet of crypto and Web3, but is true decentralization possible?

M: I think that when you say decentralization and you don't put freedom to transact and immutability—and so not being able to change that trustlessness—and privacy all in the same conversation, it sort of loses its place, because the merits of crypto aren't just decentralization. It's about sovereignty and choice and privacy and trustlessness. When you put all of those together, that's when you get proper decentralization. Using decentralized tools in a centralized way will lead to the things that we're seeing in the market now, which is explosions and frauds and things like that. Using decentralized tools that respect the way that they're built in a trustless way, in a way that allows the sovereign individual to have the choice of how they want to transact with the items and then also respects the privacy of the person—then you get a full decentralized model. The difference is about the organization of those things. Is it organized be to centralized or is it organized to be decentralized? Essentially, what you're saying is that instead of having something that comes from the top down, you have something that emerges from the bottom up, and the tools are the same, but how they're used is fundamentally different.

And so I think, yes, it's possible. It takes a sort of learning curve, a skill, to be possible. And it's not just the people building it; it is the people using it as well. So just over time, we'll see that play out. When you first went and did Airbnb, there was a learning curve for people to trust that process, right? There was a small amount of people that got it straight away that were like, "Hell yeah, I can stay anywhere! It's not a hotel. It's amazing." And then there was a whole part of the world that was like, "I will never stay in someone else's house. I do not trust that." And over time, it became this culturally acceptable behavior set. Now it's completely normal just to choose one or the other. And the same thing will happen with this technology, with decentralization, but you have to give people the time to learn to accept it as a cultural norm, to then even be able to participate in that properly.

B: So then, what about DAOs? From what I've seen so

far, even though they're supposed to not have leaders, they end up with leaders.

M: That's a perfect example of the market not being quite ready for it yet. And also even your expectations of when you say decentralization—and generally people's expectations—is everybody making decisions and everybody benefiting from those decisions. But what decentralization is probably going to look like is more of a mosaic than a group. And so what does that mean? It means that there are groups of people under a banner, which is a DAO. And those groups are each organized groups, usually between three and ten people. And in those groups, each person, like in any group or any project, has a different skill set, and different people take leadership over different activities. So there's always going to be a hierarchy of skill set depending on the other task.

So all those groups will be doing their things. And everybody decides which groups will get allocated funds from the treasury. But the actions of each of those groups are guided by individuals in different leadership positions. And they all feed back into the main thing, and then everybody benefits from it. So there's that sort of "everybody doing and everybody benefiting," but there's another layer underneath it, which is like mosaics of behavior and projects.

To take a very complex notion of thinking about how the commons work in society and that it's going to be down to a three-letter word (DAO) and that everyone's going to make every decision and it's all going to be good. That's never going to happen! What's going to happen is that slowly over time, these small groups will be organized, and it'll be much easier, because the tools will get better for the big group to make decisions to help these small groups prosper. And a DAO will look a little bit more like that. It's an oscillation between big groups and small groups that all share common goals, which are voted on by the people. And the difference there is then to say that no one single person is still making a decision, but single people in groupings like these mosaics are all putting decisions forward. And then the bigger group gets to have its say.

B: In my opinion, you are the thought leader in tokenomics. Can you explain what that means and why it has powered some of the more successful NFT collections?

M: Well, definitely we're all guessing. Anyone who's a thought leader in crypto is just taking as many educated guesses as everybody else. But I mean, tokenomics means token economics. So that can be quickly perceived as money—the movement of money as a transaction in an ecosystem. What the crypto technology does is it assigns and allows value to things that are emergent. Instead of having predetermined things that are of value, there are no predetermined things that are valuable. And what's valuable emerges from the bottom up, from the community. So a meme is all of a sudden valuable, or a picture is valuable, or a community membership or a time or space or all these things that are completely ephemeral, that have never been able to be captured and moved in and around an ecosystem. That's what tokens do. They take that kind of value, the value that you can't touch and feel and see, and they package it and they put it into a technology that allows you to move it from one place to another.

So, then what you can do is you can create all kinds of experiences and dynamics for people to take that value and move it. All of a sudden, a curator—someone that's made a choice about what they like just because it's their personal choice, and puts that into an ecosystem, and then a project—can say, "Oh I see that. That's a cool choice that I wouldn't have chosen. I'm going to give that value, so I'm going to give them something extra, with a token." All of a sudden, their curation, their aesthetic preference, something completely ephemeral, has a market value that can be transferred in the ecosystem, bought and sold by someone, moved to and from. That's what tokens do. That's what tokenomics is about. So it's saying, "What experience do you want to create in your ecosystem? And then how do you structure a set of tokens to allow whatever emerges from a value proposition to be captured and moved in that ecosystem?" So the experiences that you want to come out of it are possible over time. Is that too technical?

B: I was actually just wondering, how are you explaining this so comfortably and simply? Tokenomics, in my mind, are always so complicated.

M: It's not, it's so simple and beautiful; it's about watching what happens and then figuring out ways to just move that somewhere else through the ecosystem. It's the most simple thing.

B: One of the things I love about you is that you have this unbreakable belief in crypto and NFTs that goes beyond media FUD and champions the culture, innovation, and artistry of great work. What is your hopeful philosophy on the technology and overall space?

M: I'm sure that a lot of people can relate to what it feels like to not have access, to truly be separate from the things that you need to have a good life, to have good structures around you, to have safety, to have ownership, to have choice. I don't even think it's due to malicious reasons, but through time and embedment and many bad decisions and all the complexity that happens in society, there are a lot of things that create that gap between the people that need it most and the things that they need.

For me, the absolute fundamental merit of this technology is to be the solution for that gap. It bridges a gap of access. Anybody that has access to the internet can build with this technology. There is no gateway. There is no special qualification. You just need to be able to read. And you don't even have to read English because it's in many languages; you just need access to the internet, and even just a mobile phone. And you can build with this technology, and not just build, but you can literally open up a world of possibility, stuff that would be scheduled just for people that have degrees or connections or money or prestige.

That's system-breaking stuff. And that's so exciting. It's beyond hope. It's actually something that's real and possible and already being built. For me, I don't even pay attention to the stuff, the day-to-day stuff, the FUD, the hype, the whatever. I don't get caught up in any of it because I constantly go back to this thought of the times that I've been without, and how many people there are in the world, and how most of the people in the world are without. And how just a little bit of this can make a fundamental difference for those people.

That's it. For me, that's it. I know that I've built things that have allowed people to come onboard this technology, and their entire lives and their family's lives have been changed. And I'm no one in the spectrum of the world. I'm not anyone special. I don't have special degrees. I don't come from a special family. I just built something. And somebody else now has that capacity. None of the other stuff should matter. It's a great equalizer. That's the potential. And whether it lives up to that potential or not, we still don't know. It could go either way.

The problem with that, the flip side of absolute access, means that anybody can use it for a malicious cause. It's like freedom of speech. It's the same kind of paradox. Just as you have the freedom to say anything, it means you also have the freedom to hurt anyone and cause great damage and great harm—as much as great good can come from all the words. It's funny— the responsibility of freedom, the responsibility of this technology is that we need to get more people who understand what it means to be without, to build on it. Those are the people who actually build with this other person in mind. For me, that's it. All my focus is there. Everything that I build, all the clients that I work with, all the people that I hang out with—I'm just thinking about that. I'm thinking, "How is this going to make that outcome at least a little bit more possible?" I don't think I can have the capacity to actually meet that myself or anything, but I just maybe can contribute a little further.

B: Are NFTs a scam?

M: I mean, the T-shirt says it, so . . . I mean, they're as much a scam as anything else can be. Like, your email can be a scam. But they're also art. Even the scams are art.

B: Yeah, even the scams are art. It's true.

M: So, I'm here for all of it.

NFTS ARE RELIGION

On January 6, 2021, as insurrectionists stormed the steps of the U.S. Capitol, hell-bent that the presidential election had been stolen from Donald Trump, the nation stood by dazed and dumbstruck. Political chaos had been sown for years across Facebook and twenty-four-hour news cycles, but nothing could prepare us for the hysterical mobs scaling the West Front, infiltrating the halls in gas masks and waving Confederate flags and Trump banners. Barricades were folded, law enforcement was trampled, at least seven people lost their lives, and United States history took a hard turn.

How did this happen? The mayhem was so startling and outrageous that experts attributed the chaos to larger existential factors beyond politics. It's been suggested that many of Trump's voters and constituents share the markings of religious zealots or cultists, swearing allegiance to a leader against objective facts. It's no surprise that

Donald Trump's been compared to cult leaders like Jim Jones, David Koresh, and Sun Myung Moon throughout his regime. *Dilbert*'s creator, Scott Adams, wrote a *New York Times*–bestselling book on how Trump is one of the most persuasive speakers of our time. The author Steven Hassan of *The Cult of Trump* argues that the former president's diehards are victims of a destructive authoritarian cult according to the BITE model (behavior control, information control, thought control, and emotion control).

Sometimes I think about how much innovation and cultural progress was delayed, if not lost, during the Trump administration. It was harder to create when there were so many distracting headlines and punditry clouding our imaginations. It was tougher to break through with all the bickering and opining stealing our headspace. I don't care which side of the political wall you stood on, you've gotta admit that the public conversation was much more obsessed with national politics during that time.

And so, when the 2020 election results started solidifying and it certainly seemed like Trump would be forced to exit office, there was a thundering exhale as Americans dropped their shoulders. Group chats simultaneously wondered, "So, what do we talk about now?" It was time to get back to work, make money like dutiful capitalists, and venture beyond the maddening tumult of sociopolitical polarization. The perfect palate cleanser was the meme-stock revolution that uncoiled at the exact same time as the Capitol attacks. Americans were hunting for a refreshing gulp of cognitive dissonance from the looming death of democracy. What better way to scrape the tongue clean than with cheap, fast cash? Especially if it was amassed by ironically rallying around failing movie and video game store stocks?

As you know, money isn't enough to satiate American avarice. We're just as motivated by identity and community (or its upside-down cousin, tribalism), and the most fervent contemporary movements and trends masterfully meld them all together. The only thing that feels as good as getting rich is doing so by rallying around an impassioned cause with a band of like-minded friends. Take, for example, megachurches or social-justice-minded corporate marketing. Trump is also an illustrated example of this irresistible cocktail of branding and religion, business and politics. Stonks and meme stocks were an invigorating departure from doomsday politics, but AMC and GameStop weren't the sexiest team names to adopt. What made a lot more sense is a Reddit-powered, community-run investment movement architected around cartoon mascots, viral brands, and streetwear-styled marketing. Enter cryptoart and cryptomedia, what eventually came to be known as NFTs.

When I first dropped into NFTs, I scheduled weekly group Zooms with friends and peers from fashion, art, skateboarding, and other sectors that were curious about this burgeoning technology. I curated the rooms with people who had either expressed interest in Web3 or who I believed could benefit—and benefit from—the community.

It was hard to find reliable sources and clear education on the subject matter, so the NFT-curious resorted to WhatsApp and Telegram group chats, soaking in the material with old friends and cultivating fresh relationships with new ones. NFTs introduced me to people I'd never have befriended otherwise. I come from a streetwear past of hooded twenty-year-old dudes and here I am partaking in dinners with techies and engineers, bestselling authors and social influencers.

For those of us who fell head over heels for NFTs, there weren't enough hours in the day to explore the theories and speculate about the potential. There weren't enough conversations to keep pace with the speed of opportunity. We were from different walks of life but jointly staring down into the lush valley of a digital gold rush, which was also conveniently a haven from the black forest of COVID, crime, and climate crisis behind us. And the most striking part was how alone we were in embracing this new future. We weren't just the only ones to witness it, everybody on the outside ridiculed us (or hated us) for envisioning it. So the conversations grew even more inward and clandestine. This was the world's best secret and now some of the most intelligent, ardent, and stubborn people in the world collectively carried a point to prove.

I half-jokingly called these group-Zooms "NFTAnon," inspired by QAnon, because so much of the dynamics smelled like cult behavior. Cults are often pejoratively defined as unorthodox religious groups that practice unconventional beliefs. They are often dismissed as zealous and fanatical compared to more mainstream and institutional faiths (cryptocurrency versus fiat currency, for example). For that reason, cults like the Branch Davidians or Heaven's Gate are painted as sinister or malevolent social factions. QAnon is arguably the most notable cult in America today, orchestrated by an anonymous message board figure named Q who spawns big-tent conspiracy theories about COVID-19 and Democrat-run Satan-worshipping pedophilia rings. I was obviously using "NFTAnon" in jest, but NFTs' subversive attitude against mainstream Big Tech, the defensiveness against public scorn and media misconceptions, and the sudden, deep bonds of a devout community (that was largely anonymous) had all the markings of a cult lite.

There is one patent distinction of cults, however, that NFTAnon did not share: pledged devotion to a leader or an organization. Cults are highly focalized around charismatic founders like Osho or Keith Raniere of NXIVM and their ideologies. NFT enthusiasts, and the crypto umbrella that envelops them, don't have a magnetic figure to glorify, let alone one person's set creed or dogma to subscribe to. In fact, a chief leader, sole governance, or core belief system run counter to the foundational thesis of cryptocurrency: decentralization. Crypto's nature is to disperse power and meaning through fluid ownership and anonymity. The individual who created Bitcoin, Satoshi Nakamoto, has never been properly identified. Ethereum's founder, Vitalik Buterin, designed his blockchain "as a decentralized platform, responsive not only to his own vision but also to the will of its builders, investors, and ever sprawling community." Many blue-chip NFT founders like Yuga Labs fought tooth and nail to stay off the grid, empowering their communities to lead the fate of their projects. The very fact that you can "pump and dump" and shed loyalty to an NFT project with the click of a button says a lot about how cultish NFTs actually are (or aren't).

In fact, when you consider the vast latitude and free will associated with adopting or jettisoning crypto culture, the system around NFTs looks a lot more like the other side of the dichotomy: religion. Although many world faiths look to singular points of power (for example, Catholicism and the pope), the leading religions like Islam, Hinduism, and Buddhism operate with decentralized structures. Westernized Christianity is emblematic of decentralization, having no central office or leadership and with countless branches, factions, and sects following a spectrum of biblical interpretations.

Whenever I suggest that the NFT phenomenon feels wildly religious, I get immediate backlash from the crypto crowd. Religion, after all, is not only out of fashion to the progressive folks—and frowned upon by the intellectual set—but rapidly declining in America. In a 2019 Pew Research survey, more than a quarter of Americans identified as unaffiliated in terms of religious identity, including atheist, agnostic, or "nothing in particular." And over the pandemic, church attendance fell below 50 percent of Americans for the first time in history.

It should be noted, however, that the majority of churches closed regular worship services due to COVID-19 safety measures. In fact, there's data to support that globally, people became more religious over the last several years. Pew Research published that Americans were "far more likely" to say the coronavirus crisis had strengthened their faith, rather than weakened it. Researchers even found that online searches for the word "prayer" soared to their highest level ever in over ninety countries. Throughout history, people have turned to religion in the face of existential crises, wars, famines, plagues, and other insurmountable adversities. A global pandemic, a politically polarized landscape, impending economic fallout, even deep-space photography and evidence of UFOs, have pushed us all to ask the bigger questions. The difference today is that religiosity is climbing while faith in institutions is crumbling. Humans, as it turns out, are still searching for meaning, just not through the traditional practices, worship grounds, or long-established faiths.

One corner that humans have flocked to is technology. Over the last century, technology has been blamed for the death of religion while simultaneously being called the new religion. It's wiped religions off the face of the planet like Mikado worship after the atomic bomb dropped on Hiroshima in WWII. Meanwhile, religion is hailed as a secular substitute for theology and a tool of transcendence.

Although the contents of QAnon might be nonsensical, its existence makes sense when considering that some Americans are starved for answers and strong leadership. It's easier to believe in conspiracy theories than to accept that the experts don't know everything, and the world precariously hangs in the balance of chaos and disorder. It's harder to accept that our realities are scaffolded by mythmaking and reinforced with storytelling. To patch up the holes in the previous fictions, it's human nature to continue writing new narratives to bridge the reality gaps. QAnon, in a vacuum, is zany. But how else do you explain a single bat bringing the world to its knees or cold places that are suddenly on fire? You'll sleep better at night by blaming the "other" for your ongoing discomfort instead of chalking hardships up to Mother Nature or entropy or random chance.

QAnon also fills another glaring void in culture, and that's the absence of identity, community, and social connection. With church attendance down, employees working from home, schools closed, and the pressure to plant a flag in a time of fear-induced tribalism, it adds up that so many Americans would find refuge in shared interest groups from golfing clubs and crystal collectors to white supremacy organizations and anti-vaxxers. For the last decade, social networks like Facebook and Twitter have siloed us into echo chambers of news and opinions. But pandemic lockdowns pushed us deeper into our internet K-holes and social factions, hidden from view, tucked away together in Discord DMs and private Signal chats. For many of us into crypto and NFTs, this sounds hauntingly familiar. Even back in 2012 when crypto was first invented, the Church of Bitcoin was founded to grant Bitcoin users a nonreligious spiritual outlet and to escape oppression by existing religious groups.

Although this is anecdotal, time and again I find that my friends in this space are nursing Trump hangovers or are even societally uprooted. Not only do they feel alienated by the extremes of both political parties, they're at a crossroads in career, relationships, and marriage. Many are uncertain about where to live, whether the COVID boosters are working, and whether they should laugh at the new Dave Chappelle special. But there are some things they feel unequivocal about: blockchain technology, Web3, and anybody else who empathizes with the same vision of the next internet. It's just us now. Us against the world.

Religion is the shared reverence for the supernatural, sacred, or spiritual as well as the symbols, rituals, and worship that are associated with it.

—FRANS DE WAAL, *THE BONOBO AND THE ATHEIST*

I was raised in the Korean American Baptist church and then moved to a nondenominational mixed congregation in my teenage years. Although my Baptist upbringing was scored with hellfire and brimstone, the nearness of Satan, and the ubiquity of sin, I remember these "American" churches fixated on the constant threat of postmodernism. In his 1979 book *The Postmodern Condition: A Report on Knowledge*, Jean-François Lyotard argued that language and knowledge were changing at the hands of theorists. In the future, my youth pastor forewarned, everybody will abide by their own truths and perceptions of reality. This will not only dethrone God and compromise his sovereignty but uncork morality and social order.

I didn't see what was so bad about postmodernism. At the time, the largest criticism of the American Christian church was its absolute declaration that there was only one God, one truth, one path to eternal life.

> *I am the way and the truth and the life. No one comes to the Father except through me.*
>
> —JOHN 14:6

But it was the nineties, the season of gangsta rap and AOL chatrooms. Americans were finally waking up to diversity of not only skin color but faiths, ideologies, and religious beliefs. After 9/11 and the proliferation of Islamophobia, it seemed culturally insensitive if not racist to uphold Christianity as the only real religion when so many beautiful people from around the globe had varying interpretations of God and spirituality. Therefore, there had to be many truths, many roads to salvation.

As we've seen play out over the past decade, however, this postmodern path toward subjectivism and relativism hasn't been without potholes and speed bumps. We already had an information bias problem when there were six media strongholds controlling the news. Today, anyone with a social media account is entitled to their own facts and dissemination of truth. It's hard tackling a global virus when there are billions of opinions on what it is (or if it exists). It's also challenging to define who the president of the United States is or what constitutes human life or race or gender when everyone is wedded to their own reality. And if nobody can agree on what's fundamentally real or what's not, then there's an erosion of trust across the board.

Even on a more mundane level, we're having a rough time with fixed facts and veracity these days. StockX, a popular sneaker-reselling site, is flooded with fake shoes, some of which are so literal to the reference that even the manufacturers are having a hard time discerning the difference. Popular culture is infatuated with true-life podcasts and television dramas about scam artists and fraudulent entrepreneurs selling false products and fictitious careers. Elizabeth Holmes of Theranos and Adam Neumann of WeWork made ungodly amounts of money by committing to their own versions of honesty, even though it didn't align with anyone else's morality or ethics. And part of the reason Elon Musk wanted out of the Twitter deal was the revelation that much of the social media's user base wasn't human but fake bots. It's not just luxury handbags, diamonds, or the news. It turns out that even our societies and relationships are fake.

In his Bitcoin white paper, Satoshi Nakamoto pioneered a new technology by which a list of records—or blocks—are linked together through cryptic coding. He called this the blockchain and it was his way of confirming that there was only one truth as to what was real. And not only could you authenticate this information, but everyone else could objectively and universally agree, thereby canceling out any subjective opinion on accuracy. There's no refuting the blockchain; there is no room for interpretation.

There's a word for this: "consensus." Socially, "consensus" means there's general agreement or unanimity across individuals. In blockchain technology, a consensus protocol ensures that all participants sign off on a transaction, verifying its authenticity. Basically, the blockchain is the unadulterated, comprehensive truth. A rigid and uncompromising doctrine.

Scroll back to John 14:6. Remember, Jesus said, "I am the way and the truth and the life." In fact, the Bible is riddled with passages that refer to God as truth. He's referred to as the "Spirit of truth" in several verses, and in Hebrews 6:18, the Bible reads, "It is impossible for God to lie." Under Christian logic, if God is truth and so is the blockchain, then is God the blockchain? Maybe it's a laughable theory, but consider some other similarities between the two. The blockchain's second defining quality is that it's immutable, meaning that it can't be changed. Its permanence and finality lend to its integrity and trustworthiness. The same is also said of God in the Christian Bible: "For I the Lord do not change" (Malachi 3:6). "Jesus Christ is the same yesterday and today and forever" (Hebrews 13:8).

Across most major religions, you see the same rationale play out in defining God's characteristics. The Koran, for example, explicitly states that "God is the Truth (the Real)." And in religions that don't necessarily believe in a single God—if at all—truth is the highest degree. In Hinduism, Brahman is the Ultimate Reality, the Vedic idea of truth. Buddha's teachings, meanwhile, are broken down into the Four Noble Truths.

Most religions are founded on sacred texts with cryptic origins. God handed Moses the Ten Commandments on Mount Sinai. Christianity leans on the Holy Bible, a manuscript that was written by forty different authors over 1,500 years, all having been inspired by the Holy Spirit. Vyasa wrote the Bhagavad Gita and Mahabharata. And Joseph Smith discovered the Book of Mormon, supposedly written on golden plates by multiple prophets, buried in a New York hillside and revealed to him in a dream.

Crypto and NFTs don't have a central leader or scripture. But if they did, the most likely candidates would be Satoshi Nakamoto and his precious manifesto: the Bitcoin white paper. Only nine pages in length, Nakamoto's paper leveraged the distrust around banks and financial institutions during the Great Recession, proposing "a purely peer-to-peer version of electronic cash [that] would allow online payments to be sent directly from one party to another without going through a financial institution." The Bitcoin white paper would not just set Bitcoin up to be the first and most popular cryptocurrency in the world, it also paved the way for thousands of other cryptocurrencies. Yet both Nakamoto and the document remain shrouded in mystery. Since publishing the original thesis in 2008 and passing it around in an email group, Nakamoto has never been identified. The first sign of his existence was upon publication of the white paper. Two years later, expressing that his job was done, he disappeared from the face of the earth completely. And, as with many religious scriptures, the most prominent theory is that the white paper wasn't written by a single individual, but by a group of developers. This, especially because the blockchain code is the stroke of such genius and succinct perfection. Godlike.

With crypto, we have a divine creator that emerged from mystical origins. We also have a belief system that sprouted from a sacred text. Another hallmark of religion is the matter of the supernatural, namely the metaphysical and the afterlife—mystical concepts that are having a harder time fitting into our evolved logic and reasoning. As it turns out, NFTs and Web3 play right into this.

"Seeing is believing" has been the fundamental doubt wedged against God and religion since the dawn of time. In the Bible, "Doubting" Thomas contends, "Unless I see the nail marks in his hands and put my finger where the nails were, and put my hand into his side, I will not believe" (John 20:25). Thousands of years later, as humankind becomes more educated and materialist, the rebuttal against religious thought persists that there is no hard evidence of God. Without physical, visible, or tangible proof, it's becoming increasingly more challenging to adopt a set of beliefs on sheer faith. Society is getting only more paranoid, distrusting, cynical, and demanding of concrete, empirical data.

Our imaginations don't even run free with urban myths or playful anecdotes anymore. It's unthinkable to let a familiar song play over a café loudspeaker without Shazamming it or to allow a frivolous, friendly debate dissipate into the ether. We've got to cross-check every fact against Google to stay winning and do copious amounts of internet research to affirm our righteousness. Since we can't agree on a moral compass or universal code of ethics, we flee to search engines to enforce truth and tell us what is real. And the more points we stack in our corner to buttress our opinions, the more secure the ground feels beneath our feet. This is why we are so quick to cancel people and condemn their behavior. It's why we write off entire swaths of human beings who uphold different perspectives. For most of us, allowing outside worldviews in shakes an already flimsy foundation.

Growing up in the Christian church, the immediate defense we were provided against "I don't believe in God because I can't see him" was the wind argument. "Well, we can't see the wind, but we can see its effects. How it stirs the leaves on the trees, how it ruffles our clothes." This was a thin rejoinder when the objective sense of touch could account for wind's existence, but the point was noted. There are plenty of real things in the world that we can't see, although we can observe their influence. Physical CDs are obsolete and MP3s aren't stored on our iPod Nano devices anymore. Music instead streams off some esoteric "cloud" in the sky. Yet we appreciate the feelings and emotions that well up when we hear Frank Ocean croon. We know that our savings tied up in banks aren't physicalized as stockpiled bands of cash somewhere in a back room. Just like when we invest in stocks, it's data, not dollars. And still, we continue to make trades and keep faith in these institutions that our money will return if we call it, regardless of how unstable the economy looks ahead.

One of the strongest hypotheses for why NFTs gained so much traction over the last couple of years is because we were forced to spend more time online during lockdowns, for schooling and working from home. But it wasn't just about exposing more of our lives to social apps. Additional screen time might mean deeper addictions to tech's reward systems, but it wouldn't be enough to invoke paradigm shifts. The likeliest reasoning for this disruption is the unconscious acquiescence that our digital existence is just as—if not more—meaningful than our physical experiences.

Since AOL, we've publicly resisted the internet's slow stranglehold on our attention, even though deep down we indulge in its splendor. For whatever reason, there remains tremendous guilt and stigma with online living, so much as to call it an addiction. A shameful and dystopian aftertaste lingers, even though our phones tell us the sobering truth of how many countless hours we dedicate to TikTok and Instagram. We prefer, instead, to believe that our lives garner the most growth and purpose from real-life experiences and interactions. But through the pandemic, it became more socially acceptable to conduct our meetings over teleconferencing apps and meet up with a friend over FaceTime versus a date in a noisy restaurant. And we adapted to the new normal that just because much of our family communication is now done over ethereal texts (and not in person over handshakes and hugs), it doesn't make the relationships less substantial. People aren't less real just because they aren't physical.

Today, the coronavirus is the strongest counterargument against "seeing is believing." Viruses and antibodies are invisible to the naked eye, yet most of us have faith that they exist and are responsible for our maladies or good health. For thousands of years, we waged wars against physical threats like rival nations and tyrannical despots armed with catastrophic weapons and military might. Today, our greatest threats aren't tactile or visible. They're existential and digital: climate change, cyberattacks, contagions. The United States has responded to Russia's invasion of Ukraine with soft-power tactics like squeezing their economy. Russia has infiltrated Facebook for years, injecting our feeds with misinformation and fake news and spoiling our elections. Just because you can't see hacking bots doesn't mean they can't wreak profound havoc on a country. Just because you can't see germs doesn't mean they aren't the reason for your malaise.

As with God and religion, the persistent judgment—or jeer—against NFTs continues to be that unless they can be held, they aren't real. In a viral Instagram post, Ye (the artist formerly known as Kanye West) requested that people stop asking him to do a "fucking NFT." In January 2022, he wrote, "My focus is on building real products in the real world. Real food. Real clothes. Real shelter." Ye, meanwhile, has made a lucrative career by selling digital sounds and luxury brand names. NFT doubters and skeptics balk at the thought of paying thousands of dollars for JPEGs because we've been conditioned to believe that digital images are free and owned by nobody. Because internet art and photography haven't historically been affixed to a price tag, they're considered less serious and even unreal. But NFT traders know that—as with priceless paintings or fashion labels or other media of collectible art—value isn't always determined by hard, objective sciences. Often, the most "real" and valuable components of our lives are rooted in manufactured fictions like branding, scarcity, and Veblen goods. The price difference between a CryptoPunk and a Yeti follows the same principles between Chanel and H&M. To a layman, there might be little distinction between the products. In fact, the materials may hold the same weight and quality. The boldest difference is in the marketed myths surrounding the brand names, stories spun by influential leaders and repeated by communities. These narratives are invisible. These attitudes are air.

There are enough people in the world now who agree with one another that crypto is valuable and NFTs hold meaning and purpose to make Web3 a formidable reality. They've made something out of nothing, pulled this story out of the ether (no pun intended), and sealed the cracks by putting their entire weight behind it: personal reputations, careers, and whopping investments of money. Sounds a lot like faith. As with the religious set, people who fear COVID-19, and consumers who believe one brand's cotton is worth more than another's because of the unique narrative behind a logo, the fact that NFTs don't have physical status isn't a deterrent for the crypto crowd. In a way, NFTs' ungraspable, supernatural nature only makes it trickier to dismantle.

Are NFTs as real as the wind? Well, at least you can own them.

Crypto and NFTs are probably not a religion, but they do have religious tendencies. Nowhere is this more evident than in the virtual reality department of Web3 now known as the Metaverse.

Most religions put forth this notion of a holy destination. There is a goal in mind and it's to achieve enlightenment, a state of nirvana, or enter an afterlife. With crypto, it's hyper-Bitcoinization—the inflection point at which Bitcoin is mass-adopted to become the main global currency. In NFT land, the targeted objective is the moon. Going "to the moon" is the point at which the line on an NFT's graph shoots upward to the heavens. But there is a much greater mission associated with Web3 and it's far beyond the outer limits of space. It's even past the boundaries of Meta's Oculus VR headsets and digital real estate. The Metaverse isn't just a revised interpretation of *Second Life* and immersive video games. It's about immortality and what comes next after our physical existence ends.

Contrary to popular belief, I think the most compelling metaverse movie isn't *Ready Player One* or *The Matrix*. It's the fourth episode of the third season of Netflix's dark tech drama series *Black Mirror*. Entitled "San Junipero," the story follows two young women who find each other in a simulated playground and fall in love against a backdrop of eighties pop songs and coastal sunsets. *SPOILER ALERT* As the plot develops, it's revealed that the women are actually aged in the physical world, sick and dying. They're tapping into these simulations from their retirement homes and hospitals with the aid of an apparatus. As they die, their consciousness is downloaded onto drives and plugged into a colossal server, housing thousands or millions of other souls also inhabiting this digital planet. San Junipero is not just a virtual retreat. It's a means of living forever in the afterlife, if not a different life.

"San Junipero" was a big hit for not only Netflix and *Black Mirror* but also television as a whole. Regarded as one of the best TV episodes of 2016, it was praised for its positive take on technology, as opposed to the usual, sinister sci-fi plotlines. The idea that technology can improve the human condition and help us live forever has a name: extropianism. The prehistory of Bitcoin had a high overlap with the extropian movement, according to Finn Brunton's origin-telling of Bitcoin, *Digital Cash*. From its inception, crypto has been inspired by the potential of immortality.

Living forever is a familiar pursuit and fantasy for mankind, from the fountain of youth to antiaging creams to cryonics and advancements in health and medicine. Digital immortality, however, is a modern obsession inspired by living eternally through avatars, AI, and mind uploading. In 2007, the United States began funding research "to combine artificial intelligence with the latest advanced graphics and video game–type technology to enable us to create historical archives of people beyond what can be achieved using traditional technologies." A decade ago, the regarded futurist Ray Kurzweil predicted rapid developments in neural engineering will make digital immortality possible by the 2040s. Today, the conversation has turned on innovation in hologram tech, to memory caches and the Metaverse.

I was wearing a face mask in the spring of 2012, but it wasn't because of a coronavirus. There was a dust cloud sweeping through the main stage area of Coachella. I wrapped my head with a flannel shirt to filter the air as I eagerly awaited my first live Tupac concert experience. Tupac, of course, wasn't actually in attendance at the music festival. The late rapper had been murdered a decade and a half earlier, so a company had produced a hologram of him to perform—the first of its scale. Leaning forward against the steel barricades that balmy evening, I happened to be standing by Shakur's family members who had sat through the dress rehearsal hours earlier.

"What was it like?" I asked as the lights shut off.

"Eerie," an elderly relative replied softly. "It really looks like him up there."

As the piano started building in the background, a ghostly apparition of a bald, shirtless man resurrected from the earth. "Yeaaah," Tupac's hologram called out to the crowd, "you know what the fuck this is . . ." before rolling into a rendition of "Hail Mary" to a curious and captivated audience.

To anyone watching up close, Tupac's likeness was

unmistakably projected onto a mesh screen, in what is known as Pepper's ghost effect, an old Disneyland trick. It was hard to shake the appearance of animation, the character's movements jerky and awkward, the light reflecting off his skin with a cartoonish glint. Like eyes adjusting to a dark room, it took a few minutes for the audience to settle in, "buy into," and acclimate to the presentation. If I squinted a bit and concentrated on the music, there were brief, magical moments where I could dispel reality and Tupac Shakur came alive in front of me. And when Dr. Dre and Snoop Dogg took the stage in person and interacted with the hologram, it enhanced the illusion of a complete performance.

The Tupac hologram was an amusing experiment that didn't strike much of a lasting legacy. There have been other attempts at deceased-rapper holography since from Eazy-E to Ol' Dirty Bastard, but the virtual performers have turned into a carnival stunt. The art and technology aren't fully realized yet, leaving just enough doubt to dismiss the concept wholesale. In fact, it looks like it'll be a while before we stack the computing power and resolution to achieve true CGH (computer-generated holography). Even still, we don't totally believe. Life and consciousness are sacred and miraculously bestowed, either by science, the universe, or God. It's almost offensive, if not sacrilegious, to mirror humanness through shabby augmented reality gimmicks. And no matter how convincing the deepfake renderings are and how indistinguishable the holograms may be from the reference, there's always a small part of us that knows we are being bamboozled by modern-day ventriloquism.

And still, we want to believe. Before their breakup, Ye gifted his wife, Kim Kardashian, a hologram of her late father for her fortieth birthday. Robert Kardashian dons a tan suit and a full head of hair as he tells Kim how proud of her he is and how her husband is "the most, most, most, most, most genius man in the whole world." Emotional, Kim tweeted that the present was a "special surprise from heaven" before adding, "It is so lifelike!"

In a viral 2020 news story, a Korean woman wears a headset to be reunited with her seven-year-old daughter in a virtual environment. Na-yeon, the daughter, succumbed to a disease three years earlier but is seen running around a garden in a purple dress and a Disney *Frozen* purse.

She pops out to ask, "Mom, where have you been? Have you been thinking of me?"

"Always," the mother replies tearfully. In the video, she then cries, "I really want to touch you just once. I really missed you."

The digital reunion is heartbreaking to watch, and some may even find it disturbing. But for both the engineers behind the project and the mother, the technology is a warm and beneficial tool that can help a lot of people. The mother goes on to say that she was happy to see her daughter through the medium. A few months ago, the company behind the production, Seoul-based VIVE Studios, raised a $9 million investment for more metaverse activations on a consumer level.

Web3 is the one arena where VR, AR, holograms, and the Metaverse are all converging. It's not just about bringing the dead back to life, however. It's also about life after death. The fact that NFTs exist on the blockchain forever already adds a layer of gravity and spiritual depth to the experience, but there are also multiple projects in the works that expound upon the afterlife and immortality. Somnium Space is a metaverse company that is selling a function called Live Forever, where your digital clone acts as an eternal avatar on their platform. The creator was inspired to build Somnium Space after the passing of his father and the realization that they'd never be united again. By aggregating data and personal information on an individual, and incorporating artificial intelligence, Somnium Space re-creates them in a metaverse where friends and relatives can visit and engage with them.

As with the Tupac, Na-yeon the Korean daughter, and Robert Kardashian holograms, however, the discrepancy with Somnium Space's digital avatars is that although they enable the living to engage with a copy of the deceased, it does nothing to help the referenced subject. These people are long gone and their souls and consciousness aren't inhabiting these digital bodies, the way they are in San Junipero. This would require intricate facsimiles of your brain. In a 2016 *Atlantic* piece entitled "Why You Should Believe in the Digital Afterlife," the author Michael Graziano writes, "You would need a scanning device that can capture what kind of neuron, what kind of synapse, how large or active of a synapse, what kind of neurotransmitter, how rapidly the neurotransmitter is being synthesized and how rapidly it can be reabsorbed. Is that impossible? No. But it starts to sound like the tech is centuries in the future rather than just around the corner."

Even if and when we get there, there's a larger wave cresting right behind this one. "Is it truly conscious, or is it merely a computer crunching numbers in imitation of your behavior?" Graziano's without an answer here and it's the conundrum that continues to frustrate the argument for a digital afterlife. We will eventually be able to re-create your brain, loaded with your personality, emotions, and experiences, in a hyperrealistic depiction of your body in a simulated environment. But is it really you?

On Thanksgiving weekend 2021, the esteemed designer Virgil Abloh died in Chicago, Illinois. Virgil's passing was sudden and shocking to most everyone, as the Chicago-born artist had kept his illness and ensuing struggles private. In the days and weeks following his death, his legions of fans, friends, and peers worldwide began sharing their favorite Virgil mementos across social media. There were pictures of valuable Nikes and Off-White fashion pieces Abloh had designed. People posted his book, photographs of him DJing at a party, and sage quotes. What was remarkable about the Virgil Abloh tributes, however, were the screen-grabs of thoughtful text messages, DMs, and comments that he'd strewed to his worldwide community. We began to realize just how much he had communicated with all of us. Virgil was constantly interacting and engaging with people through his apps and everybody cherished these personalized moments. It didn't matter how famous or important you were, he took the time to acknowledge your messages and notes.

Because of the amount of time he invested in these connections, much of our relationship with and definition of Virgil was digital. And because so much of his work was either mediated over the internet or showcased on social channels, our understanding of his contributions was also virtual. The digital afterlife is a lot easier to wrap your head around when you take into account the digital life.

It's therefore not totally unreasonable that on most days it feels like Virgil Abloh is still very much alive. Today doesn't feel any different than this day one year ago, where Virgil's latest collaborations are inundating my feeds, his interviews are replaying on YouTube, and he was somewhere distant in the galaxy, hammering away at the next brilliant handbag or assembling his next museum exhibition. Sometimes there were long stretches between texts and messages; perhaps he's on a break or maybe we just don't have much to talk about right now. I'll see him again backstage at the next fashion week, I tell myself. Or he'll tap in when a memory arises. I'm sure we'll collaborate on something for our next food festival.

In the meantime, Virgil's art continues on in the Metaverse, influencing and inspiring us endlessly. His creations are his avatar and we are the blockchain and we resoundingly and unanimously agree on him.

THE STREET DOES
NOT REALLY EXIST

In the summer of 2021, I wrote this essay to map out my reflections on NFTs and how they could enhance our lives. By default, I look at most new technologies through the lens of a brand builder and business owner. "How can this innovation disrupt my art and how can it resolve any friction in our process?"

As I articulated my thoughts on Web3, decentralization, and a new way of considering the brand-consumer relationship, I realized that I'd homed in on the purpose and meaning behind The Hundreds' foray in the NFT space. What transpired became the Adam Bomb Squad white paper. This manifesto not only introduced the world to our Web3 philosophy but onboarded scores of newcomers to NFTs. The year 2021 was the Wild West where creators were dreaming beyond borders and shooting for the moon. Today, many of the hard ideas I cooked up here would be under heavy scrutiny. In the months after I published this paper, the government ramped up securities and regulatory talk around NFTs because they were behaving more like stocks (offering utility or the speculative promise of a future reward) than novelty collectibles (which don't claim to be anything beyond what they are). Truly, the biggest question surrounding the fate of

NFTs (as we know them today) will be answered by the Securities and Exchange Commission as time goes on.

If you've watched the Woodstock '99 doc, you know it's less an analysis of music festivals than it is about displaced male rage and the anxious social climate as we teetered on the new millennium. The year 1999 was an awkward time for the world; it very much felt like we were neither here nor there, nervous about what Y2K might bring (or take). Or maybe that was just me, as I turned nineteen in the year 1999. Not quite ready for the responsibilities of my twenties yet feeling distant and removed from my youth. That same year, a movie called *The Matrix* premiered in theaters, architecting a cyberpunk universe around virtual reality and a classic hero named Neo. Keanu Reeves plays an average dude who jacks into the simulation and is reborn a Christ figure. Once he acknowledges his departure from the physical world and embraces his standing in the green grid of ones and zeros, the possibilities are limitless. At the time, with the dawn of the internet, many young people shared Neo's enthusiasm and ambition around this brave new world. We were graduating from AOL chatrooms and finding each other on ICQ. And then a website called Blogger launched in the late summer of '99 and changed everything. Once again, maybe the entire planet didn't feel the ground shake, but I certainly did. "Blog" is short for "web log" and it was a means to broadcast loud messages and connect with a borderless audience. Blogger addressed a lot of the problems that plagued traditional media. For one, it was relatively free and decentralized (not governed by the Big Six media strongholds). Blogging was also efficient, immediate, and lowered the barrier of entry for desktop publishers. After years of cutting, gluing, and pasting physical zines at Kinko's to distribute to one hundred punks at my local music venue, I could now blog to thousands, and then millions, of strangers from Detroit to Indonesia. In fact, I saw so much inherent value and opportunity in blogging that when Ben and I started The Hundreds four years later we framed our clothing brand with the technology. Throughout history, fashion had been storytold exclusively through product and advertising. Blogging (and its later iteration, social media) changed that, erasing the line between logos and lifestyle, design and narrative.

We were one of the first clothing companies in the world to capitalize on the power of a dynamic web. In the early 2000s, a start-up T-shirt label from L.A. called thehundreds.com was attracting as many eyeballs as a Gucci HTML page. Most fashion designers used their websites to publicize a CONTACT US button or static lookbook. They rarely updated their dot-coms. Meanwhile, you could refresh The Hundreds' front page two to three times a day and be surprised with fresh material. The hyperactivity of our blog communicated streetwear's galvanic energy to an impressionable new customer. This first generation of the internet (Web1) also granted independent brands the freedom and power to circumnavigate gatekeepers and media middlemen. In those days, it cost $10,000 to take out an ad in *Complex* magazine. Through blogs, upstart designers like The Hundreds without any connections, clout, or money could now tell their story in their own words and meet customers on their own terms.*

For the next ten years, blogging and social media amplified and expedited our mission in streetwear. Then the rest of the brands caught up, thanks to centralized Web2 applications like WordPress and Instagram. In the decade and a half since, this marriage of blog and brand has become business and revolutionized how companies and commerce perform. Yet there has been relatively low innovation otherwise with regards to both fashion and technology. On the tech side, the platforms swap out and e-commerce gets more sophisticated, but we've become complacent with the system and stagnant with the breakthroughs. We've acquiesced that this is the internet in its final form when the truth is that Web3 is just beginning. The next evolution of the internet—NFTs, blockchain—is inspiring and stimulating me in a way I haven't felt since Blogger launched twenty years ago. And a lot of that excitement has to do with, once again, a revised approach to fashion.

THE METAVERSE

Although the concept has been floating around for some time, the science fiction writer Neal Stephenson coined

---

* I should clarify that the technology wasn't the key component that brought The Hundreds to the world. For the blog to work, it required a writer and a photographer and, most importantly, someone who saw the benefits of tending to a community and cared enough to do it. Most technology can't replace the creator's ideas or intent. However, technology can accelerate an artist's vision.

the term "Metaverse" in his 1992 novel *Snow Crash*. "Hiro's not actually here at all. He's in a computer-generated universe that his computer is drawing onto his goggles and pumping into his earphones. In the lingo, this imaginary place is known as the Metaverse."

Ever since, futurists and blockbuster movies alike have referenced the term for a reality that is tethered to both a digital and a physical experience. In *The Matrix*, Neo is immersed in a fantasy world of red dresses and bending spoons while physically wired into a postapocalyptic dentist's chair. The Metaverse is different from solely virtual reality and it's not necessarily a game or an internet thing. It's this idea that there is a universe beyond (a.k.a. "meta") the one we've known and participated in. In this Metaverse, rules are being written, societies are being built, and new realities are being constructed.

"When Hiro goes into the Metaverse and looks down the Street and sees buildings and electric signs stretching off into the darkness, disappearing over the curve of the globe, he is actually staring at the graphic representations—the user interfaces—of a myriad different pieces of software that have been engineered by major corporations."

The working theory is that we will build atop the tech to mirror our lives here in the physical world. There will be no hard line drawn between this reality and the next. One day it will hit us that we have already been living a full metaverse existence, one where our physical and digital lives are inextricable and unmanageable without the other.

For many of us, that awakening was the pandemic. It wasn't just food delivery apps and streaming services that made the lockdown transition more seamless than it would have been a mere years ago. While Zooms handily replaced meetings, our social relationships stayed intact because our friendships are hoisted up by digital rebar. There are many friends I haven't seen in five months, ten years, or decades that I maintain an unbroken rapport with virtually. Some of these people I've never met in person at all! And yet we've shared deep conversations in forums, worked together over DMs, and built memories in group chats like any other IRL relationship. It wasn't long ago that we defined friends as online or "in real life." Today, that distinction is evaporating.*

Not only is our social life already grounded in the Metaverse, so is much of our identity. Last year, we used filters to alter our appearances, posted black squares and blue stripes to declare our political stances, and farmed carrots in *Animal Crossing* to feel productive and purposeful in a flat and motionless season (all while binging *Tiger King*, prostrate on the couch in tie-dyed sweatpants by a DTC brand). In the Metaverse, we can be whoever we want, unfettered by physical constraints, geography, even race, class, and gender. Video games allow unlikely athletes to be e-sports champions. Editing apps bless those with beauty. In Ernest Cline's *Ready Player One*, Aech's avatar in the OASIS is a white heterosexual male. In the physical world, Aech's name is Helen Harris, a Black lesbian. As the world around us decays and grows more inhospitable—whether due to climate change, pandemics,

---

* Spike Jonze's 2013 movie *Her*, in which Joaquin Phoenix's character builds a romantic connection with an AI that he'll never encounter in his physical life, doesn't seem so outlandish in the year 2021.

political differences, or social collapse—the Metaverse becomes more enticing as a refuge.*

If you can accept that we're already steeped in the Metaverse, that our bodies remain in the physical world while our brains are increasingly minding a digital life (are you having trouble concentrating on your dinner date, anxious to return to a developing conversation or situation on your phone?), then it only follows that there needs to be some type of protocol to establish ownership, goods, and property in cyberspace. The apt currency to trade in this galaxy of virtual worlds are crypto coins like Bitcoin, Cardano, and Doge. My sons call Ethereum my *Star Wars* money and it certainly sounds like something Watto barters for on Mos Espa. Planet Earth has been slow and cautious in accepting Jedi cash, so in the Metaverse, NFTs are commodities and utilities to spend cryptocurrency and accrue value with digital investments. Even my grade-school sons appreciate how a fistful of Robux (*Roblox*) or V-Bucks (*Fortnite*) enhances their life over a twenty-dollar bill at Target.

THE ENVIRONMENT

Speaking of which, we should probably start by discussing why humans need to own anything at all. At some point, we went from cavemen with no possessions, to hunter-

* The thought leader Balaji Srinivasan talks about pseudonymity in the Metaverse (the ability to commandeer multiple identities and profiles) as a foil to cancel culture. Whereby canceling one of your pseudonyms doesn't take down your entirety. You can simply pivot to another avatar and continue your life and livelihood.

gatherers, to hoarders stashing sneakers and rare vinyl. We own some things for utility and survival. Then there are those items that are imbued with sentiment and fill an emotional need. We also own things to decorate our lives, to make our environment more tolerable or beautiful. And we hold on to much of our possessions because they express who we are. In his book *Subculture*,* Dick Hebdige talks about how punks upset the wardrobe with antiestablishment symbols† to fight the hegemony.

It's hard to judge which pieces of property are essential. How do you weigh the necessity of an heirloom against an appliance? But you can debate their costs and detriments, especially when it comes to the environment.

Look around. Chances are that you have too much stuff. I've spent the last two weekends editing my closet of clutter and feel like I've barely made a dent. It's a problem that weighs on my mind, considering the type of work that I do. I run a streetwear clothing brand here in Los Angeles. We've generated truckloads of T-shirts, denim, baseball caps, and jackets. And although we're doing what we can to repurpose apparel via a vintage program (Greatest Hits), incorporate recycled water and cottons in production, and employ sustainable materials, there is no doubt that we contribute to gratuitous waste. The sustainability

---

* If there was a bible upon which The Hundreds is spiritualized, it's probably *Subculture* by Dick Hebdige. Although published in 1979, I didn't discover the book until—you guessed it—1999!

† "There was a chaos of quiffs and leather jackets, brothel creepers and winkle pickers, plimsolls and paka macs, moddy crops and skinhead strides, drainpipes and vivid socks, bum freezers and bovver boots—all kept 'in place' and 'out of time' by the spectacular adhesives: the safety pins and plastic clothes pegs, the bondage straps and bits of string which attracted so much horrified and fascinated attention."

question is a real thorn for the fashion industry because if you look only at the utility aspect of apparel—to protect us from the elements and insulate us from exposure—then we have enough clothing to last us a lifetime. No matter how environmentally conscious brands are with their manufacturing, the very existence of new fashion is problematic in an unforgiving, black-and-white world.

Many are making it look as if the fashion industry are starting to take responsibility, by spending fantasy amounts on campaigns where they portray themselves as "sustainable," "ethical," "green," "climate neutral" and "fair." But let's be clear: This is almost never anything but pure greenwashing. You cannot mass produce fashion or consume "sustainably" as the world is shaped today. That is one of the many reasons why we will need a system change.

—GRETA THUNBERG, CLIMATE ACTIVIST,
VOGUE SCANDINAVIA, AUGUST 8, 2021

The type of clothing I design and make is especially prickly because it's artistically, socially, and identity driven. I believe in the virtues of art and design and how fashion can make people feel happy, special, and part of a community. But is there a way to accomplish these functions without taxing the environment and exacerbating the climate crisis?

This is an awkward reentry point for the metaverse

conversation as the computers that house simulated environments and mine cryptocurrency transactions devour energy at an alarming rate. Although Bitcoin mining is starting to clean up its act and Ethereum is transitioning the blockchain to a proof-of-stake system, even Elon Musk rescinded his crypto cosign earlier this year because of its environmental impact. Bitcoin's network, according to *Fortune*, "uses more power per year than Pakistan or the United Arab Emirates." Of course, there is the rebuttal that any and all computer activity harms the planet. "The average impact of a user on Instagram is 18.6 $gEqCO_2$/day, the equivalent of 166 meters traveled by a light vehicle." And back to fashion, making one T-shirt eats "up to 120 liters of water per wear, and contributes 0.01 kilogram of carbon dioxide per wear, just from dyeing alone." This, before you factor in the energy costs to print, the chemicals in the ink, and shipping and freighting these T-shirts between factories and to the end-consumer. Oh, and then there's what happens to the T-shirt once it dies . . .

Since we're ruminating on a fantasy world, let's indulge a bit and imagine a future where crypto carries through with its promise to run cleaner. The Metaverse could solve many of fashion's environmental issues and maybe it already does. Consider the blue "verified" check, a badge of distinction. The real-world equivalent might be something akin to a friends-and-family pair of AF1s, a Rolex watch, or a medal of honor. In 1974, Umberto Eco wrote, "Not only the expressly intended communicative object . . . but every object may be viewed . . . as a sign." Donning a graphical logo in your profile picture is not unlike hanging it on your back. They are both acts of affinity, announcing your association with a lifestyle to your friend group. Except one of these things projects and the other pollutes.

A "GOT 'EM" screen-grab off Nike's SNKRS app holds as much weight as wearing the sought-after shoes to a party. Most of us who are fashion-aware could tell you all about Kanye's GAP "round jacket," the levitating puffy coat having flooded our feed enough times to commit to memory. Yet we've never seen one in "real life," considering the actual jackets aren't even made yet. Meanwhile, the coveted pieces are just as ubiquitous as illuminated pixels as they would be stretched across reams of nylon. Billboard-size projections of the jacket are currently blasted onto the sides of buildings in New York, Chicago, and Los Angeles.

In a more direct and literal sense, brands are already designing clothing for the Metaverse. The social status aspect of fashion is on the move from cotton to pixels. Video games have been doing this for years. My children are well-practiced in shopping for digital outfits in games like *Fortnite*, more conscious of their *Valorant* skins than the types of T-shirts they wear on the playground. Shops like BNV.me, artists like Stephy Fung, and sneaker brands like RTFKT are creating and selling metaverse fashion that run parallel to what you might find stocked at Dover Street Market. Before his death, Virgil Abloh hinted that he was working on dressing you for the next world with the help of the venture capitalist and essayist Matthew Ball. It's only a matter of months before the social apps flip the switch on for NFTs. Just like you can pull a Disney princess filter over your face in Stories or Snapchat, you'll be able to wear your favorite digital sweatshirt on TikTok. There will be an IG tab to showcase all the NFT art you've collected with the capabilities to trade them on the blockchain. (NFT art can stand for everything from a motion graphic to a scan of an oil painting to a pair of Bode shorts.)

THE FUTURE OF FASHION

Having said that, on the topic of metaverse clothing, what excites me the most is not the mirroring of physical garments in the virtual world. It's thinking beyond the confines and constructs of logistics and tradition and norms. This is where I envision NFTs and the Metaverse really changing the game. There are two prongs that will drive the future of fashion:

1. the reimagining of design and
2. the rethinking of brand and business

For as long as I can remember, I've kept a copy of the *Codex Seraphinianus* on my desk. Published in 1981, the *Codex* is a meticulously detailed encyclopedia of a fantasy world, illustrated and told by the artist Luigi Serafini. Included are colorful drawings of bizarre food eaten in this imaginary space, wedged between chapters of made-up ecosystems and fabricated science. Even the text is comprised of a fake language that Serafini distills down to an alphabet and vocabulary in the appendix. While the creatures and customs are reminiscent of our world, Serafini designs the plants and chemistry beyond the scope of our earthly limitations. In the fashion chapter, the garments could dress the cast of *The Hunger Games* or *Alice in Wonderland*. Flashlights project out from the chest, umbrellas are worn as hats, and shirt sleeves loop infinitely into themselves.

While fashion has been pinched and pulled for centuries, the useful innovation has stayed within the parameters of human anatomy, legal and ethical boundaries, and the laws of physics. In the Metaverse, our avatars don't have to play by any of these rules. (Note: In *Snow Crash*, Stephenson stipulates that "your avatar can't be any taller than you are. This is to prevent people from walking around a mile high.") Not only can we identify with the gender and weight we feel most comfortable with, but we can also be cartoon trees, bored apes, or a foggy orb wrapped in bacon. If one of our pseudonyms is a purple duck, then physical-world shoe design won't accommodate our webbed feet. A COVID face mask won't fit our wide bill. And do pants go over or under our feathery tail? This sounds silly, but you can see how traditional fashion can quickly fall obsolete when the template for design centers around a slender, proportionate European male or female with two arms and legs. If you add a seventh arm or a second head, how does that impact the garment's silhouette, where to draw emphasis, and the way the fabric drapes? Do you need to wear shoes or belts in the Metaverse if gravity doesn't apply? Do you need clothes at all if there are different thresholds of nudity? What if you aren't a corporeal being?

Because exposure and weather are less of a dire concern for clothing in the Metaverse, there is an accent on the social function of apparel and accessories. On the other side of the screen, fashion will be more about identity, tribalism, status, and self-expression than ever before. The difference is that those statements won't be relegated to a T-shirt graphic, a red hat, or a pin on a lapel. Like a Plumbob in a *Sims* game, that signifier may come in an oscillating pink diamond hanging over your head. Fashion doesn't have to just be dresses and jackets anymore. Fashion can be polka-dotted skin, thirty-seven rabbits circling you like a hula hoop, or a liquid sweater that's eleven miles wide.

THE FUTURE OF BUSINESS

While we're rethinking fashion design, we should also take another look at the business behind it. As I write this, I'm wearing a pair of Brazil Dunks. The Nike swoosh is one of the rare logos I wear like a uniform, even though I am not friends with the founders and do not get paid by the company to promote for them. I believe that Nike executes superior design and aligns the best partnerships. Yet my unquestioned loyalty to the swoosh sometimes makes me think back to wearing large skate logos on oversized T-shirts as a teenager.

"You look like a walking billboard," my mom would remark. "Why do you want to advertise for some corporation that doesn't care about you?"

Of course, the answer was nothing more than, "Because it's cool, Mom. You'll never understand!" But the further explanation was that I felt like I was a part of a lifestyle and subculture by wearing that logo. A "Think" tag or "New Deal" graphic was a quick ID on a core, authentic skater. With my brand, The Hundreds, we've also sold a similar meaning behind our logo and mascot, Adam Bomb. Young people from around the world have proudly sported the cartoon to exhibit their ties to streetwear, love for Los Angeles culture, or empathy with The Hundreds' point of view.

Beyond the usefulness or quality of a product, people commit to brand names because of three things:

1. Identity
2. Community
3. Sense of ownership

Yet, while wearing Nike tells the world something about my identity, and while dressing in The Hundreds offers our customers a community, neither of us retain any skin in the game. That disparity in ownership betrays a big disconnect in the brand-consumer relationship, one that until now has been dismissed because there was nothing to be done to fix it.

When I first started delving into NFTs, what most intrigued me was the postulate that social media companies have made 100 percent of the revenue off the creative content that its users publish on their platforms. This explains why these corporations have become the biggest—and their founders the wealthiest—in the world. Twitter generated $3.7 billion in revenue in 2020, an 8.8 percent increase year over year. Meanwhile, Facebook's advertising revenue was $84.2 billion (they've more than doubled since 2017). Everyday creators know their work has value. They've just been convinced over the last decade that there isn't a market for their art or ideas and that the clout associated with posting free content is just as valuable as currency.*

Designers and clothing companies also hold a disproportionate relationship with their patrons in that the customers advertise brands without being compensated equitably. Travis Scott catches a check from Nike because the culture deems him an influential person. But every time I wear the "Check over Stripes," I'm a Nike influencer too. In fact, anyone who has a following—whether you have six hundred people on TikTok or three people who admire your shoes at the barbershop—is an influencer. Nike shouldn't pay us equal royalties for helping them move product (Travis sells millions of sneakers, while I've maybe convinced my dad to grab a pair of Monarchs on sale), but if there was a device that could measure an influencer's impact and grant them some of the upside in a brand's success, then everybody wins. The consumer is incentivized to wear the company's product because they now hold all three cards: identity, community, and ownership. And the brand gains greater visibility in the marketplace.

---

* Plus, there just weren't many viable solutions on centralized platforms to be compensated for content (subscription sites like OnlyFans have experienced rapid growth in response).

ADAM BOMB SQUAD

Along with Blogger and *The Matrix*, there was one other seismic development in 1999: Napster. The peer-to-peer MP3 sharing software broke the music industry, which up until that point bottled music in $12.99 plastic discs, distributed from behind a monolith of big-box retail. Once the floodgates torrented open, the fans reclaimed the power in the label-listener balance. They dictated how music should be consumed: quality singles, instead of paying for eleven shitty tracks. Music became more discoverable and shareable. Napster's greatest legacy, however, was in taking music online.

Whenever friends of mine have trouble grasping the intangible nature of NFTs, I point to music. As a borderline boomer, I still have trouble discarding my CD wallets and cartons of cassettes, even though there's no stereo in my car or boom box at home to play them. I'm still emotionally bound to these jewel cases and liner notes, but it's time that I accept that music has been invisible for twenty years. We don't even store files anymore, we stream sounds off a cloud, whatever that means. Napster was instrumental in this paradigm shift—in how the business around music is conducted, but also in how music is received and enjoyed.

SYSTEM CHANGE

In *Snow Crash*, Neal Stephenson's metaverse is called the Street, "a grand boulevard going all the way around the equator of a black sphere with a radius . . . considerably bigger than Earth." The author later clarifies, "The Street does not really exist—it's just a computer-graphics protocol written down on a piece of paper somewhere—none of these things is being physically built."

The world I come from, streetwear, also traces its origins to a hypothetical street. Although we dawdled around the Lower East Side and lined up in Harajuku, even though we hang our hat(s) on the Rosewood corner of L.A.'s Fairfax District, the "street" in "streetwear" is code for the cultures and subcultures that fostered us. The "street" can take the form of a BMX track, a sunset wave, or a sneakerhead message board.

Before COVID took hold, there was a lot of discourse around the state of streetwear in end-of-decade editorials. The 2010s had witnessed an underground fashion movement seize the mainstream spotlight. Streetwear was Everywear: on everyone and everywhere. Louis Vuitton's Virgil Abloh predicted in a *Dazed* interview that the party wouldn't last: "Its time will be up. In my mind, how many more t-shirts can we own, how many more hoodies, how many sneakers?"

I kinda love the narrative that the first NFTs were Larva Labs' CryptoPunks because the original U.K. punks circa 1979 also challenged and reshaped fashion's definition. Eventually, punk style became too popular and played out, just like streetwear's overexposure. In Hebidge's terms (from *Subculture*), it's to offer streetwear new meaning:

Thus, as soon as the original innovations which signify "subculture" are translated into commodities and made generally available, they become "frozen." Once removed from their private contexts by the small entrepreneurs and big fashion interests who produce them on a mass scale, they become codified, made comprehensible, rendered at once public property and profitable merchandise . . . Youth cultural styles may begin by issuing symbolic challenges, but they must inevitably end by establishing new sets of conventions; by creating new commodities, new industries or rejuvenating old ones.

Greta Thunberg did call for a system change . . .

A couple of weeks before Virgil's quote in *Dazed*, I also proclaimed that streetwear was dead, but in the sense that it's constantly culminating and renewing: "The streetwear generation is about regeneration." The takeaway from this essay echoed my memoir, *This Is Not a T-Shirt*. Streetwear is boundless because the ethos exists beyond the clothing. It's beyond the pavement and beyond . . . the physical. All things considered, at this juncture, doesn't it make the most sense for streetwear to dress the Metaverse?

"Streetwear transcends dress and music, just like rock 'n' roll set the philosophical tone for an era. Streetwear defined a generational attitude toward art and commerce, brand-building, and financial autonomy. It was like punk, but about selling. It was like business, but not about selling out.

"'Streetwear.' Over the next ten years, perhaps we'll call hoodies and hats something else, because 'streetwear' will be applied to tech . . ."

Is Metawear too . . . meta?

THE HARDEST YEAR

In August 2021, on the morning of peak NFT activity for the year, The Hundreds minted out Adam Bomb Squad, our first PFP-style set of twenty-five thousand digital collectibles featuring Adam, Badam, and Madam Bomb. Within hours, celebration and relief careened into Discord maintenance and customer support for anxious collectors. What transpired over the next year and a half would be one of the most demanding, confusing, and challenging seasons of our business, but in the end, we emerged with an invaluable lesson.

Trevor McFedries of Friends With Benefits taught me about NFTs in 2020 after I asked him about a newsworthy auction he tweeted. In December, Beeple sold twenty digital artworks as The Complete MF Collection, netting $3.5 million. It took me a few weeks (and several Zoom sessions with Dee Goens from Zora) to wrap my brain around owning digital art on the blockchain. It wasn't until January 2021, however, when Gary Vaynerchuk put me onto CryptoPunks, that I grasped the significance and power of PFP collections. PFP-style NFTs are like unique, one-of-one trading cards in a limited-edition set. Their collectors use the NFT as their social media avatar to not only express their identity but claim membership to a tribe.

"Do you have a CryptoPunk yet?"

"What's a CryptoPunk?"

"Punks are it."

Gary isn't long on texts. But I'd ignored his advice on several regrettable decisions before. Before the pandemic, he insisted that I plunge into basketball cards.

"Like, old ones? My brother collected Hoops when we were kids."

"Any," he responded.

"Like, anybody at all? Or like, Lebron rookies, that sorta thing?"

"Go on eBay and buy anything. Shaq's rookie card tripled in the last week. Old cards, new cards, whatever you like."

By the following year, those cards were commanding tens, if not hundreds of thousands of dollars. I never know if Gary is right or if he just makes it right. It's probably a combination of the two.

So (my partner) Ben and I went shopping for a Crypto-Punk. Created in 2017 by John Watkinson and Matt Hall, CryptoPunks are ten thousand JPEGs of pixelated, 8-bit-style character heads that are largely unremarkable— and indistinguishable from one another—to a layperson.*
Some wear 3D glasses, are cloaked in a hoodie, or smoke

---

* Unsurprisingly, given the demographics of the crypto space, the brown and Black Punks are disproportionately weighted to the floor (meaning, they have lower demand and therefore lesser resale value). It's hard to tell if this is out of innate racism or because people buy Punks that they identify with and use to represent themselves in their avatars. Of course, this theory doesn't hold water considering how esteemed blue alien Punks are . . .

a brown pipe. Others have orange beanies and blue bandanas or messy red hair. There are male and female Punks, but also creatures like gorillas and zombies.

For the last several years, Punks waded through a crypto drought. There weren't many eyes on Bitcoin or Ethereum after 2017 and even less interest in trading twenty-four-by-twenty-four-pixel pictures on the blockchain. Ten thousand NFTs was a fat supply for just a few hundred people who truly cared. So when the pandemic dropped NFTs and crypto back into the rotation in late 2020 and suddenly hundreds of thousands of people around the world were joining Clubhouse rooms to learn more, ten thousand was not nearly enough. In the coldest demonstration of supply-demand economics, Punk #5822 initially sold for $14 in 2017, then a few thousand bucks a couple of years later. After the NFT boom, it went for a couple million in early 2021 and fetched over $23 million one year later.

Most popular trends are kinda absurd and stupid if you aren't entrenched in the mechanics of the culture. My favorite music genre is hardcore but I don't know why anyone would listen to the rasping cacophony if they've never attended a live show. Twenty years ago, I remember how people used to laugh at young men for collecting footwear the way "that women do." If you were regularly chatting on the NikeTalk message board, hanging out at downtown street boutiques, or reading Japanese fashion magazines, it made all the sense to invest in rare trainers to help differentiate yourself from the rest of the uncultured sheep wearing bad shoes. Context is king. When I first read that Beeple's digital artwork was fetching millions of dollars, I was confused, angry, and threatened. The more I learned about NFTs, however, their value at auction made just as much sense as blue-chip paintings or overpriced handbags or exotic cacti.

The Punks game is all about collectability, cool, and scarcity and that was a science we'd mastered, if not influenced. And by "we," I mean sneakers and streetwear culture. From *Star Wars* figures to vintage Levi's, oil paintings to sports cards, people have always cherished and hoarded precious artifacts. Streetwear, meanwhile, infused a tincture of relevant culture and youth lifestyle trends with collecting. Like punk or hip-hop, lining up for a sneaker release is now a legitimate youth-driven subculture. Reselling sweatshirts on apps has become its own micro economy. It started off with creating, then it was about collecting, and now it's about capitalizing. Punks felt very parallel to rare streetwear and sneakers to me, but without the physical effects. They also reminded me of basketball cards because of how fun they were as a trading hobby. And the buying/selling exchanges happened so frequently, and the gains and losses could be so consequential, that the best way to follow their path was through hard data and graphs—just like day-traded stocks.

As Ben and I grazed through the Larva Labs marketplace, the only strategy I could summon was that the closer a CryptoPunk resembled a punk rocker, the more authentic it probably was and had perhaps the best crack at longevity and sustainable value. Sucks to be me: turns out this isn't how the game is played at all and our mohawked CryptoPunk languished in our wallets for a few weeks before we flipped him for one wearing a purple hat.

Purple hats were trendy because Gary Vee said so. I think we paid about $20,000 for the NFT at the time and the lesson to not take everything so literally—or linearly—in NFTs was priceless.

No surprise, the market on CryptoPunks dramatically dipped not long after we bought one. I've never been a reseller or a stocks trader, so this brought on crippling anxiety. When I was a kid, my dad taught me about mutual funds and my angsty retort was that this was just legalized gambling. The more he debated me on it, the more I dug my heels in. The way I saw it, buying things to have and use was smart and ethical. Buying things with the intent of selling them one day for a profit—otherwise known as "investing"—was irresponsible and sinful. You buy a house to live in it, not because it might appreciate in value.

When streetwear culture shifted in the late 2000s to optimize reselling, it felt viscerally unnatural. Kids weren't buying Supreme because they respected the design, quality, or storytelling behind the brand and product. They were waiting in line for hours just to purchase a few items, walk them up the street to a secondhand store, and dump them for a quick profit. Streetwear and sneakers went from being treasures to transactions. This is what happens when you boil everything down to money.

There was no way I could let Gary Vee know I was scared, so I mildly asked him his thoughts on the market. He was doubling down, saying that the slump was temporary and the cheapest CryptoPunks would be at least $100,000 by the summer. I wasn't comforted, so I called up my friend Nick and expressed my fear. What if we lost everything on this JPEG? I'd feel like a moron.

"Nick, we just bought this Punk and it's already losing value. What do you think we should do?"

"You're fine. But if you're ever uncomfortable with it, I'll buy it from you."

"Seriously?"

"Yeah, I have no doubt that they're gonna blow up. I have a buncha them. Just lemme know."

It was that sense of conviction that separated the losers from the winners. How could Nick have so much faith in these NFTs? I'm sure Gary knew of significant moves behind the scenes that were driving the market, but still, nothing was guaranteed and he was inhaling CryptoPunks like they were potato chips. Partially because of Nick's standing offer and partially because we were too lazy to do anything about the purple-capped Punk, the NFT sat in our wallet. Mere months later, by the summer of 2021, CryptoPunks had a $100,000 floor.

As Ben and I got more enthused about the CryptoPunks and the dynamics around their ecosystem, we reached out to Matt and John at Larva Labs and inquired about doing an official collaboration together. The way we saw it, this was a cultural milestone and arguably the first physical moment where crypto and streetwear overlapped. In honor of the purple hat trait, we made exactly that: a purple snap-back baseball cap. Our initial idea was to have various punks embroidered across different headwear styles, but Matt and John were adamant that we only use a zombie CryptoPunk and produce an extremely limited supply of hats. To no one's surprise, they sold out in a sliver of a second.*

I started writing a lot about NFTs that spring of 2021. For one, I was captivated by the space and wanted to talk to as many people about it as I could. Secondarily, there was a real lack of literature on the subject matter, especially in a digestible language for someone who wasn't technically versed in crypto. The pandemic was in full boring mode. People had nowhere else to be except on their phones or playing *Animal Crossing* on their Switches. And paradigms were shifting. NFTs were exploding, everyone else was making absurd amounts of money, and the average person was desperate for someone to package the concept for them in a tidy little box.

I moved from Clubhouse to Twitter Spaces, adjusted my social media to be more oriented around NFT talk, and hosted weekly invite-only Zoom sessions to answer questions for frustrated friends. I was drowning in stacks of texts daily, many from people whom I hadn't talked to in years. They didn't even need to mention the words "NFT" or "Web3." I knew exactly what they wanted—and of course, they assumed they were the only people in the world who'd thought to knock on my door.

"Hey man, it's been a few years. Was wondering if I could take you out to lunch sometime. My treat. Wanted to pick your brain about something . . ."

"Bobby! Do you have time for a quick call?"

---

* And we made a lot more enemies than we did new fans. Thousands of irate comments by Punks who missed out on the cap flooded our feeds, DMs, and email. To this day, many of the Punks won't touch our brand for having broken their hearts.

"Got an idea where we can both make money. You're gonna love it."

Most took offense when I said there was a line of people ahead of them or that I had to focus on my own work or tend to my family. It was also difficult to weigh a stranger's generous request to pay for my thoughts with a cup of coffee when agencies were offering $100,000 for an hour. Suddenly, I was a bad friend, selfish, and caring only about money. I had to stop checking my texts for weeks at a time and hope that the relationship would remain intact after the cyclone passed. A friend told me, "Don't worry about burning a bridge. They'll always come back when they need something again."

Meanwhile, over the last two years, I've been fielding inbound requests from famous and powerful people solely with regards to NFT advice. Never in a million years did I think I'd have access to A-list movie stars, studio executives, billionaire founders, presidential candidates, and philanthropists (and this is still happening daily). The texts and DMs are always sheathed in an anxious and nervous husk, because (1) they don't really know what they're talking about and (2) they feel like they're being rendered irrelevant. These important figures weren't curious about Web3. In fact, they didn't even know what they didn't know. They just deduced that there was something big going on and for the first time in their careers, the train was leaving the station without them. Nobody wants to feel stupid, and furthermore, no one wants to be left behind.

In response, I comforted people that they weren't missing out on anything at all. It was the truth. We all know people who didn't have a homepage in Web1 or log on to

Instagram in Web2 and turned out okay. I consulted Seth Rogen for a bit about NFTs. He felt like he was supposed to do it sheerly because his fans kept asking him about it. But the deeper our conversations ran, I could see the light leave his eyes. Seth wasn't interested in the speculative, gambling nature of NFTs, which was fair. I could see him pondering what to do. One foggy morning, the actor was staring out the window at the mist canopying his forested backyard (somehow, Seth transported a piece of his native Vancouver to his Hollywood home).

"Seth, you can also not do any of this." It's like I swung a hard left on the freeway. We'd been talking for at least two hours about all the reasons why Seth should sign up for a MetaMask wallet. He's a big art collector, and smart contracts support artists by ensuring they get a cut of secondary sales. His fan base of bearded, stoner men were also right up NFT alley, but it was like trying to convince my kids that anchovies are delicious. The more I described and defended Web3, the less appealing it sounded.

He turned his head. "I don't have to, do I?"

"Nah. In fact, the most common advice I give to people who are as dubious or just unready as you are is: 'Wait.' There's no rush. Web3 is here to stay, so let the infrastructure build a bit if it'll make you feel better. Or also, just never do it at all. Who cares?"

Seth exhaled a sigh of relief, and his warm laugh filled the room. It was like watching him unload ten thousand pounds of bricks off his shoulders.

I'd blogged for five years by writing my own HTML code and uploading a new webpage every night through an FTP server. Then, the blogging platform WordPress was born and saved me hours of time and headaches with a streamlined backend. Not long after: Twitter and Instagram innovated microblogging on smartphones. There was plenty of time for Seth to onboard to Web3. There are thousands of developers around the world hammering away at the UI/UX (user interface/user experience) for a more intuitive, smoother, and safer space. It'll be years before Web3 will be mainstream enough for easy mass adoption (it can also very well not happen). So Seth could watch from the banks and leap into the river when the timing and purpose made sense for him.

My word of caution is to avoid trends like crypto and NFTs if you're diving in solely because everyone else is doing it. The only meaningful and sustainable approach to Web3 is to genuinely care about the tech, subject matter, and opportunities. Like any trend, the hype is bound to fade and move in ebbs and flows, so invest time only if it's a niche you foresee long-term work in. Seth Rogen didn't need more money and his eyes are set on filmmaking, ceramics, and weed. Of all the people I've talked to about NFTs, he proved to be one of the smartest about his Web3 strategy—by staying out of it.

I started experimenting. The very first NFT I minted was on Zora. Dee Goens (the marketplace's cofounder) walked me through all the steps of setting up a crypto "hot" wallet (a digital storage of my cryptocurrency and NFTs) and plugging it into my Google Chrome browser. He told me I could mint whatever I wanted as an NFT on the blockchain—anything at all. Photos, graphic designs . . . I could even claim words or letters. That morning, I think I saw RAC or 3LAU secure "fuck." I dipped my toes in by grabbing the bomb emoji. Ben minted the hamburger. Then, we waited for a tug on the line.

I completely forgot about our NFTs until a couple of days later when Dee messaged me, "Have you seen your bids?"

Oh! Those email notifications were being funneled to a different inbox. There were a few bids rolling in. One was for about $3,000 in ETH. Then there was a bid for 7,777 DAI. I googled "DAI" and learned it was a cryptocurrency with a one-for-one exchange rate against the U.S. dollar. That didn't seem right. Someone out there was trying to buy my bomb emoji for almost $8,000? I didn't even design the graphic, nor did it take time or creativity on my end. I've worked on elaborate art projects for weeks that have garnered far less. It kinda made me upset!

"No, that's a real bid. It is essentially $7,777 USD," Dee told me over the phone when I asked him to look at my Zora profile. "I would accept that before it's too late."

I wasn't going to stick around to see if a better offer came knocking. I took the bid, and within moments, my hot wallet was bloated with digits. Could it happen again? I wrote an essay about stonks and my foray into NFTs and it spread well online. If I could sell an emoji or a letter, what about a few thousand words? Days after I minted my essay, there was an offer for 2,222 DAI by a new bidder. I should've been ecstatic. (The last time I was offered this much per word was when I was a freelance magazine writer pre-9/11. In college, I was churning out thousand-word music reviews by the hour for a buck a word. Those were the halcyon days of print publishing!) Instead, I was disappointed. I'd spent an afternoon writing my piece and genuinely cared about it, but the market was valuing it for less than half of my bomb emoji. Of course, like most free market dynamics, it's complicated trying to determine why or how people place value on most anything at all.*

I'm not a gambler. Decades ago, when we used to exhibit The Hundreds at fashion trade shows in Vegas, I spent $20 on a jackpot machine and watched the money evaporate like an arcade game. It felt tantamount to throwing my cash into an incinerator. There was no thrill or recreation in the activity, just stress and regret. But if I had struck $7,777 with the first pull of the lever, I probably would've chained myself to the slots at that casino for the rest of the night. I've watched most of my friends dabble in this space by minting or buying a couple of NFTs and gradually watching their crypto circle down the drain. They never come back. Fortunately—and unfortunately—for me, my first hit was a euphoric high and it propelled me deeper down the rabbit hole.

NFTs were working and their energy was expanding as news circulated of higher sales. Early NFT artists like FEWOCiOUS and Snowfro, and veteran artists like Jen

* It took me a while to register that whoever bought my bomb emoji may have confused it for our actual trademarked logo. That would justify the high bid. Regardless, it was my rookie card, so that also may have accounted for something.

Stark and Mad Dog Jones, captured daily headlines on high-end gallery-type marketplaces like SuperRare, Rarible, and Nifty Gateway. It wasn't a matter of whether their art would sell. It was about how much it would sell for.

Beeple's $3.5 million sale in 2020 was extraordinary, but within months, he sold an NFT for $69 million at Christie's. Other artists were casually making millions off their mints. In the same March of 2021 that Beeple sold "Everydays: The First 5000 Days," the DJ 3LAU released a collection of thirty-three NFTs to commemorate the three-year anniversary of his *Ultraviolet* album. Although the weekend-long auction should've closed out around $1 million as anticipated, 3LAU gamified the ending by restarting the clock every time someone placed a new bid. In what came as a surprise to everyone, the auction reset forty times with the final number tallying $11.7 million.

Matt Colon, 3LAU's manager, lives on my street. Some friends were over at my house for drinks, but I couldn't focus on my guests as my texts with Matt escalated. Every few minutes, my phone stirred with another sensational update. Two million. Three million. What the hell was going on? By the time the auction ended, I was standing outside my house barefoot, drunk on wine and wonder. I congratulated Matt and then called Ben to share what had just happened. As I took a seat on my porch and talked into the indigo night sky, I was enthralled and inspired by 3LAU's sale. It wasn't only about the staggering price. It showed that there were enough people who believed in this thing to make it alive. Money doesn't make things real, but it gets people to pay attention. Even if, as happened by the following morning, they're hating on the entire thing.

"Who would ever pay millions of dollars for an NFT? And why?!"

That's one of the most frequently asked questions about NFTs, but it's one that's never taken up too much space in my head. For one, I come from streetwear where it's normalized for grown men to empty out their piggy banks for some old basketball sneakers or a T-shirt with a trendy logo on it. For the last several years, I've also been immersed in the blue-chip contemporary art world and seen much more face-melting sales happen for pieces and artists that no one expects. If you're not in the business of manufacturing and selling goods, especially luxury items, you probably assume that prices are dictated by materials and labor. But, of course, they aren't. On the purveyor's side, there are the intangibles woven into the commercial product like rarity, brand mythology, and sheer arbitrary inflation if they have a strong enough hold on the market. On the purchaser's side, final price can be a result of bravado or social statement. There are emotions involved in how much people pay for things. Their bid can also be a product of pastime or entertainment, convenience, or charitable support.

If somebody wanted to pay 3LAU $11 million, it could be a for a number of reasons beyond being a fan of the art or hoping it would resell for a profit one day. Maybe the buyer was motivated to inject confidence in the market and onboard more converts. Maybe the buyer ran a fund and this was a strategic investment in 3LAU as an artist and innovator. In fact, by the end of the year, the DJ raised $55 million for Royal, a Web3 music platform that allows fans to scrape royalties off their favorite songs.

Whenever someone channels Seinfeld by asking, "Who aaaare these people?" the answer is that there are a lot of unfathomably crypto-wealthy men living in basements around the world who bought Bitcoin at a penny. For the last ten years, they've had nowhere to spend that money, and now, they have a playground of art and collectibles that they can spray and pray at. Eleven million dollars is pocket change if you own billions of dollars in Ethereum. Especially if you believe that the investment might reward you down the road.

You must know something about NFTs in this window of time. In 2021, the goalposts weren't just moving daily, they were shifting by the hour. Trends and truths didn't stick for more than two weeks at a time. Self-proclaimed experts fell flat on their faces. Inspiring leaders were exposed to be bigots or scam artists. Trustworthy projects crumbled as rugpulls and fast money turned into past money. If you didn't sign on to Twitter for a week, you could miss out on the entire story arc around a sensational NFT collection. Everyone was in a rush to find stable ground and plant their flags into guaranteed bets, hard definitions, and scientific conclusions about NFTs, Web3, and the Metaverse. But the earth was still soft clay, vulnerable to the next pioneer's footprints. Rules were erected, adopted, and torn down constantly with little fanfare.

It was like we discovered a new continent abundant with resources, but only a handful of people from around the world knew how to get there. This Great Valley was ripe for its own government, businesses, leadership, and even physics. Anyone could move here and be the highest acclaimed artist or most popular influencer. Better than rewriting history, you could wipe it clean and write the future. The best way to put it is that we hadn't unearthed a new territory, we were creating it from scratch.

In the first quarter of 2021, the energy and climate around NFTs were powered by one-of-one art by artists like Tyler Hobbs and XCopy and even celebrities like Lindsay Lohan and Snoop Dogg. Although NFT collectibles like NBA Top Shot were making noise, NFTs' biggest talking point at the time was that there was finally a way for artists to collect a royalty on their secondary sales. The art system has forever smiled upon the wealthy flippers and not the young creators who break their backs. Collectors, galleries, and auction houses wind up making the most money in selling the art, whereas the creator doesn't see an upside on any of those later sales. The blockchain fixed that, whereby the artist could set and receive a slice of the secondary sales on their pieces forever. Therefore, NFTs in this period were best appreciated as digital art like a Banksy versus a collectible like a Pokémon card. And as with most art, there was also no expectation of deeper utility or ancillary purpose behind the NFT. The inherent value was in owning and observing it.

Then, as it goes with NFTs, everything changed. In late April, a PFP collection called Bored Ape Yacht Club (BAYC) entered the chat and would disrupt how people considered NFTs forever. Created by Gordon Goner and Gargamel and an anonymous collective of men (who would later be doxed by BuzzFeed), BAYC was a collection of ten thousand cartoon monkeys adorned with an array of paraphernalia. Every NFT shared the same base character art, but the accessories and attributes were multifarious from white fur to vintage war helmets to biker's vests. These traits were uniquely assorted for each NFT, slapped across the ape in various permutations like a Mr. Potato Head toy. Although the BAYC formula was not so unique from prior PFP collections like the CryptoPunks, Hashmasks, and CryptoKitties, there were two glaring distinctions.

First, to accompany the project, the BAYC team published a "road map," delineating forthcoming milestones like limited edition merchandise (this included our collaboration together [The Hundreds X BAYC] and a subsequent NFT collection called Mutant Ape Yacht Club). In September, BAYC issued a second, illustrated road map of the Apes' home: a soupy green swamp in the Everglades. Around the map were hints of even loftier developments like a Miami clubhouse and a DAO. The "road maps" aroused speculation and incited enthusiasm in the marketplace as it ensured BAYC's NFT holders that the Apes weren't a flash-in-the-pan collection. Bored Ape Yacht Club was taking a stand as a serious business in a burgeoning industry that was overrun with anonymous amateurs and plagued with rugpulls. Those long-term proclamations instilled trust and conviction among the community and put pressure on other NFT collections to follow suit.

This marked the beginning of the "Wen Utility?" moment in NFT history: What could your NFT offer beyond mere aesthetic value? Smart contracts enabled NFTs to accomplish things traditional art could never achieve. So why treat NFTs the same as a flat canvas? They could do so much more, like unlocking exclusive merchandise, or being playable in a video game or swipe-able as a membership card to a private club. For the next half year, NFT collections scrambled to gamify their JPEGs, offering usefulness in metaverses like Sandbox and Decentraland, air-dropping additional NFTs, or allow-listing spin-off collections.

Yet the elephant in the room was the futility in utility. Although never expressly stated, for many collections, the demand for utility was actually more about the promise of utility. Because with the promise of utility, there was an injection of hopium among buyers, which triggered a fleeting pump in trading activity. Only recently in this bear market has it become indisputable that many—if not most—NFT traders never cared for the actual utility of most projects. When a project called Cool Cats announced that they were working on a video game, their floor prices soared to make them one of the most expensive blue-chip projects in the space. The theory was that people anticipated the game to have a positive reception when it released, raising the profile of their investment. Most successful video games take years to develop, but Cool Cats developed theirs in months. Even still, the market quickly lost interest, the Cats' community disparaged the team behind the project, and the floor imploded. By the time the game debuted, relatively few holders played it and even fewer talked about it. Regardless of the game being fun or not, the collection was flamed—not for delivering a faulty utility, but for losing control of its floor price.

Maybe it's because I come from a different generation and collect things to have them (versus profiting off reselling them), but the utility feature rarely incentivizes me. What made Bored Ape Yacht Club remarkable was the artwork. Most PFP-style NFT collections at the time channeled retro video games with 8-bit characters. If they were hand-drawn, the illustrations were basic and rudimentary to accommodate the computerized generative process. It was easy to see how the graphic layers rested atop the base template. But with the Apes, not only was the art superior, but the artist Seneca crafted intricate traits in such a way as to make each monkey look individually hand-drawn. It's funny. NFTs started off being about the arts, yet that became eclipsed by rarities and ETH score. But when you look back at the highest-priced projects in the market, the one thing they all have in common is that the art is exceptional.

BAYC's second distinction that reshaped NFT collecting was its supposed transfer of commercial rights. Up until Bored Apes, the general rule was that the purchase of an NFT was like buying art. The only right that passed from the creator to the buyer was the right to display the work. However, on the Bored Apes website, Yuga Labs' terms of use articulated, "When you purchase an NFT, you own the underlying Bored Ape, the Art, completely." In the third stanza under Ownership, the website reads, "Yuga Labs LLC grants you an unlimited, worldwide license to use, copy, and display the purchased Art for the purpose of creating derivative works based upon the Art ('Commercial Use')."*

By the fall of 2021, Yuga Labs' Bored Apes had fast become the loudest collection in the space and the one to watch over Larva Labs' CryptoPunks. Bored Apes went Hollywood. Celebrities like Jimmy Fallon, Stephen Curry, Snoop Dogg, Justin Bieber, and Gwyneth Paltrow flashed their Apes on their socials. During NFT.NYC week, BAYC's pop-up retail shop attracted lines down the block while Larva Labs didn't host an event. Although the CryptoPunks had always reigned supreme, the Apes' dogged community held fast and zeroed in on the throne.

The Bored Apes were out to prove a point. Matt Hall and John Watkinson of Larva Labs, the founders of the CryptoPunks, had built their collection four years prior, before NFTs were "a thing." As artistic engineers, their

---

* One paragraph is not nearly enough runway to flesh out every interpretation of the legal language, so what's ensued since has been one of the most confounding and complicated debates in Web3. To some in the NFT space, BAYC's terms for its NFTs have been construed as CC0, or "Creative Commons," which essentially means that the intellectual property is let loose in the public domain for others to do whatever they want with (Moonbirds, another big project, recently pivoted to this structure). The *Mona Lisa* is an example of CC0 art that belongs to the world. But this not only means that BAYC's parent company, Yuga Labs, surrenders ownership over the art, so do the holders themselves. The art belongs to no one and everyone. The Bored Apes are not CC0 though because the terms don't state that Yuga Labs passes copyright ownership of the art on to the NFT holder. Furthermore, Yuga emphasizes that they are the licensor, the entity that decides who gets to use the artwork. Thus, they retain control of the Apes.

The popular thought (for now) is that anyone holding a Bored Ape NFT is granted a broad license to capitalize off that specific artwork commercially and in content. As a result, holders have been producing derivative artwork using their Ape and marketing their own businesses around the cartoon. There are now fast-food restaurants, beer and weed companies, TV shows in development, and music groups that either incorporate collectors' Apes or showcase them as part of their branding. There's even a website called Bored Jobs where you can bid on licenses across categories for people's Apes.

NFTs were a blockchain experiment and weren't intended to compete with the utility-bearing, CC0-minded Bored Apes. The Apes' community pushed the unofficial rivalry anyway. It's only unfair when you compare, right? Soon enough, the Punks community grew irritated that they didn't own the intellectual property rights to their NFTs the way the Apes had it. It also drove them mad that their prices weren't moving as dramatically as BAYC's. By year's end, the unthinkable happened. On December 22, 2021, BAYC's floor price flipped the CryptoPunks (the cheapest Ape was higher than the cheapest Punk). The Apes had won by stamping a cold truth: in order to have a successful NFT collection, you've got to play by BAYC's rules—utility, rights, metaverse, art, all of it.

We knew nothing about utility or road maps when we started devising our own NFT collection, Adam Bomb Squad. And that's because it was still February 2021, over two months before Bored Ape Yacht Club was born. Instead, Ben and I were inspired by CryptoPunks in building out our set of digital collectibles. The Punks were valuable simply because they were the first NFT collection on the blockchain and there wasn't enough supply at ten thousand to satisfy the demand. There were no loud proclamations of developments or theoretical road map promises of add-ons. What you saw was what you got. The community hatched their own lore around certain traits and devised their own system and science around trading mechanics.

We also came from collector culture. It probably

started with my love of *Star Wars* figures, comic books, and licensed *Garfield* merchandise in the 1980s. For over half of my life, I've been collecting Bearbrick figures from Japan, out-of-print skateboards, ceramics and crystals, rare books, and art, both street and blue-chip. I had also been actively trading sports cards over the pandemic and was part of Topps' Project70 collaboration program in customizing vintage baseball cards. But above all, I was attracted to NFTs because it was clear that much of the game was inspired by our wheelhouse: sneakers and streetwear. From drop mechanics to rarity and exclusivity to luxury allure, NFTs were fashion without the cumbersome production and physical waste of clothing.

To make my case, I Instagrammed a doctored SNKRS app screen-grab (that read, "Got 'em?") and wrote about how sneaker collecting had been divorced from physical goods and reduced to digital transactions. Although my hot take wasn't happily received by sneaker culture, I wasn't making a judgment, just an observation. When I'd gotten into "retros" at the turn of the millennium, the novelty of vintage basketball shoes was in wearing them. Over the years, because of scarcity and the advent of auction websites like eBay and Yahoo! Japan, sneaker reselling became a profitable hobby. In the last couple of decades, Nike capitalized on the resale market and apps like StockX and secondhand stores like Flight Club accelerated sneaker flipping like stock trading. These days, many consumers don't even open the shoebox, let alone wear them, before they ship the sneakers to the StockX facilities in Detroit.

To save on the carbon footprint of fabrics, oils, and

gas, wouldn't it make more sense to subtract the physical product from the equation? And if the end consumer wants to keep and wear their shoes, they can exchange the NFT for the goods. (By the way, this was also the premise of an innovative NFT start-up called RTFKT, which was simultaneously happening at the time and was acquired by Nike at the end of the year for an undisclosed sum.)

NFTs addressed many of the problems we were looking to solve at The Hundreds. At the close of my memoir, *This Is Not a T-Shirt*, I write about how the tallest hurdle for streetwear is the question of sustainability in the face of climate change. Fashion is responsible for 10 percent of the world's waste, yet there's not much of a solution in sight outside of popularizing secondhand clothing. Even if companies like Patagonia commit to using cleaner resources and biodegradable resources, they are still manufacturing more of something we don't necessarily need for functional purposes. At this point, the only reason to buy more clothing isn't to protect you from exposure, it's to signal your identity and employ self-expression. And that's something that NFTs can aptly handle—as your static profile pictures or as 3D avatars moving about a metaverse.

My book—and The Hundreds itself—is a story about how brands are best when powered by a community. Yet the largest hypocrisy is that when fans support their favorite clothing companies they are shilling for someone else's business without seeing any favorable upside as the brand excels. For years, I'd praised my community, telling them that they were a part of the brand, so that they could feel a sense of ownership in our growth. The naked truth was that they kept spending the money while we kept collecting it. Not everything has to be about money. In fact, money can often distort and muddy the fan relationship. But NFTs were a means by which the art could appreciate in value if the brand grounding it gained notoriety. And theoretically, if fans of the company owned the art, then they too could benefit from widening brand recognition.

At the very least, we knew that NFTs were an efficient means of "tokengating," unlocking special product, content, or access to parties just for people who hold those NFTs in their wallet. In the future, I foresee many membership reward programs operating off blockchains, so why not have your pass feature unique and valuable art? If people held our NFTs, they could access private rooms in our Discord, but also have more interactivity with others in The Hundreds community, including myself. And again, now it wasn't just about them supporting a company or its leaders. It was about them using NFTs to establish relationships among one another and working together to lift all boats.

The Hundreds was already minting NFTs at the top of 2021, but just one at a time. To ease our community into crypto, we started off with T-shirt graphics. We released our spring collection of designs as static artwork on the Zora marketplace and the following season, animated the graphics to mimic tees drying in the wind on a clothesline. Most of the bidders were longtime The Hundreds fans who were already invested in crypto and happy to partake in this next chapter of collecting. One in particular had grown up in San Diego and was excited about purchasing one of our first NFTs. But it was her boyfriend who reached out to talk to us. His name was Allen Hena.

When I first met Allen Hena, he was a Black Crypto-Punk with a purple hat and red clown nose. All I knew was that he was an authoritative personality on crypto Twitter and had amassed a bit of a following, respected as much for his insight on NFTs as he was for his biting opinions and hot takes. He pulled no punches and had no problems calling ruggers out on their shit or critiquing bad projects. So, when he started hitting up both my Twitter and The Hundreds', he caught my attention. We got onto a Zoom and the first thing I noticed was that Allen wasn't a far cry from his Punk avatar. He was a light-skinned Black dude in an orange Reese's Peanut Butter Cups T-shirt and a trucker cap. Allen is sparing on warmth and compliments and he doesn't waste any time.

"I wanna let you know that I don't know anything about The Hundreds—but my girlfriend is apparently a big fan . . ." It turns out that one of The Hundreds' T-shirt graphics was Allen's girlfriend's first NFT, so it piqued his curiosity. Although Allen was entrenched in the space, she hadn't expressed interest in any other digital art. This NFT, however, meant something to her. "I gotta say, though. I looked into your smart contracts and you guys are doing it all wrong!"

Allen put our NFTs under a microscope, advised us on how we could better enter the space, and earned our trust. Then, after hearing a bit of our story, he let us know that if we were ever interested in creating a full-scale NFT collection, he could help us. Allen had played a part in the Hashmasks project, a pioneering collection of 16,384 unique digital portraits created by over seventy artists around the world. So he had a grasp on rarity structures and community dynamics. From writing the smart contract that backed our NFTs on the blockchain to helping ready the art, he'd walk us into Web3 properly and get The Hundreds to be one of the first brands to find meaningful placement in the ecosystem. Starting in February 2021, we met with Allen semiweekly over Zoom to figure out what The Hundreds' first NFT collection would be—and what it would center around.

Our subject was right under our noses: Adam Bomb and his counterparts, Madam Bomb and Badam Bomb. While most collections spotlighted cartoon animals and aliens and grim skeletons, nobody had centered a project around a friendly bomb.*

---

* Back in the mid-2000s when The Hundreds was starting, we didn't have a logo or icon. In fact, we barely even incorporated "The Hundreds" wording on our T-shirt designs. Heavy branding and dominant logos weren't on-trend at the turn of the millennium, and so most T-shirt brands relied on conceptual graphics and provocative designs to sell. Some of our best-selling tees read "Hip-Hop is Dead" with fallen emcees like B.I.G., Tupac, and Big L on the back. Another shirt called "Self Offense" was a drawing of a gun where the barrel pointed back at the shooter. Until we moved the market with strong art, we didn't have the clout to sell off name alone, let alone an esoteric emblem. But over the seasons, we watched as customers walked into streetwear boutiques and skate shops specifically asking for us by name. When it came time to design an icon to embody The Hundreds' spirit, I was inspired to go up against the timeless classics like the McDonald's "M," Nike "Swoosh," and the Apple logo. What made these designs so memorable and impactful was their simplicity. To me, the best logos are ones that can be drawn by a five-year-old in a few basic steps and I wanted a design that you could tell belonged to us, even from a mile away.

The Hundreds' earliest themes were "Los Angeles Lifestyle and California Culture" as well as our subcultural backgrounds growing up on the West Coast in the eighties and nineties. The visual language of the era was informed by mascot-led breakfast cereals and Saturday morning cartoons. I mean, in kindergarten I learned how to draw by tracing *Garfield* comic strips and reading *Calvin and Hobbes*! So for our first icon, I riffed on Warner Bros'

Adam Bomb has been our beloved and world-renowned mascot since The Hundreds' third year in business. As one of the most ubiquitous characters in streetwear history, Adam Bomb has graced the highest billboards in Times Square, been tattooed on rappers like YG and Travis Scott, and been highlighted in Pixar films and Netflix shows. Badam Bomb is the villain in Adam Bomb's universe, although he isn't necessarily evil. He's just misunderstood. His drooping eyes may not be red because he's stoned. Perhaps he just has bad allergies (could it be that his bandanna isn't gang-related, it's a cold compress because he has a headache?)! Madam Bomb is Adam's friend and potential love interest. All three characters share the same color scheme: black, white, red, and yellow. This was intentional because of my love of Mickey Mouse and the rest of Walt Disney's work. (Those also happen to be the four primary colors that children automatically gravitate to and that are most effective in marketing.) Together, Adam, Badam, and Madam comprise the Adam Bomb Squad (also a riff on the Mickey Mouse Club).

Over the last two decades, Adam has been interpreted

Looney Tunes (especially the Wile E. Coyote and Road Runner segments) and drew the silhouette of a classical cartoon bomb. The shape was circular and familiar, but offset by a jagged spark. It felt confident and anxious at the same time and summarized The Hundreds' vibes succinctly.

After the initial success of the Solid Bomb, Ben walked by my desk at my old apartment and suggested that there be an anthropomorphic version of the icon, since I loved drawing cartoons so much. So I stayed up and sketched different renditions of a comical bomb, landing on one with a mouth agape, concerned eyes fixed on the burning wick. In the spirit of a community-led brand, I published the drawing on my blog and asked our supporters to suggest a name. The following day, I had hundreds of emails in our inbox, calling out names like "Bombby Hundreds" and "Bomb Boy." But the clear winner was proposed by two people from different parts of the world: "Adam Bomb."

hundreds of different ways through seasonal The Hundreds T-shirt graphics. We've iterated Adam as fruits like Pineapple Adam, Watermelon Adam, and Strawberry Adam. He's been rendered as a paint smear, tattoo flash, and a stained glass design. Adam Bomb has been dressed in an assortment of hairstyles like mohawks and pompadours. He's shared every emotion as Confused Adam, Bummed Adam, and Dead Inside Adam. Adam has also heavily collaborated with some of the world's most prolific artists like Mister Cartoon, Kenny Scharf, Joshua Vides, and Blue the Great. While most NFT collections follow a formula—a boilerplate character with rotating, computer-generated traits, The Hundreds was housing a trove of original, hand-crafted Adam Bomb art in its library. So we dedicated our first NFT collection to Adam Bomb Squad and a history of The Hundreds' timeline. Each Adam, Madam, and Badam in the set would therefore be accompanied by an essay of its origins and personality, doubling as an education in the brand.

One of the countless lessons skateboarding and hardcore taught me in my youth was that passion preceded fashion. If you weren't committed and contributive to the culture, you'd fast get sniffed out, called out, and kicked out. There was nothing more humiliating or reputationally offensive than being labeled a "poser." So much of youth subculture is about credibility and being cosigned by gatekeepers, which is really about earning your stripes. There's no greater school of hard knocks when it comes to this stuff than street culture. Streetwear is guarded by outer rings of validators that run from the cool guys on the block all the way up corporate kingdoms like Nike.

So, when we entered crypto culture in 2017,* it was requisite that our motivation was not just spurred by making money, but also by a genuine care for the tech, decentralization, and being additive to the growth and progression of the culture. Crypto gelled appropriately with The Hundreds in that we're emboldened by challenging systems and questioning the norms. At its essence, crypto was about taking power out of the hands of a tyrannical few and restoring control to the people.†

* All the way back in 2017, there wasn't much cultural framework around cryptocurrencies. So we dipped our toe in by accepting crypto payments for clothing in The Hundreds' online shop. This was relatively forward-thinking for the time, especially in the streetwear marketplace, so we only got a smattering of orders from crypto-sympathetic customers over the first several months. Bitcoin and Ethereum crashed soon after that and suffered a long winter until 2020. We were such novices at this that we lost the keys to those payments and considered it a wash (and a fun first experiment).

† In my memoir, *This Is Not a T-Shirt*, I talk about the grand opening of The Hundreds San Francisco in March of 2008, which was the same month that Facebook hired Sheryl Sandberg as COO. In photos of our opening night after-party at the Clift hotel bar, you can spot Facebook president Sean Parker in the background, who just happened to also be there celebrating the social network's achievements. By the end of that year, Facebook turned cash flow positive for the first time, and the next tech renaissance washed over Silicon Valley as The Hundreds gained a cultural hold of the Bay.

You'd think that at some point, because of the physical proximity between our worlds, those streams might converge: tech and streetwear. But for the next ten years, we ran alongside each other in parallel play. It's like we were two different movies playing in side-by-side theaters. And by the end of our lease in the Bay, we knew it was time to leave when skateboarders and fixies weren't mashing down S.F.'s treacherous asphalt hills, but software engineers and VCs were commuting up them on electric skateboards.

When Snapchat cracked Venice open on the outskirts of Los Angeles, it finally seemed the moment when Silicon Valley and Silicon Beach would connect. The simplest way to look at it is that the Bay had the tech and L.A. had the culture and the smart ones would find a way to bridge the gap. Yet even the Snapchat glasses and AR filters couldn't help package tech in a sartorially appetizing way.

The word "crypto" is more off-putting and alienating than "tech" and "finance" combined. But with NFTs, there is a favorably "cool" human ingress to financial affairs and innovative technology. NFTs are about new art by emerging artists, wealth equality, and, above all, community—not necessar-

Just because NFT dynamics borrow so much from streetwear, doesn't mean that the streetwear community was sympathetic to NFTs. Although the synergies made sense to us, the hardship was not just in getting our people to be curious and excited about buying digital art on the blockchain, but to be informed, educated, and secure in participating. First step, to get our community interested in the topic, I had to advertise my zeal for NFTs, just like I've done for decades with streetwear.

In guiding entrepreneurs on brand-building, I first teach them to identify their impassioned purpose, and then to be sharply expressive and communicative to their audience about that reason why. People are attracted to passion like moths to a flame. A charismatic leader who honestly voices their intent can inspire hundreds, thousands, and even millions of people to look in their direction. The most efficient way to convince people to explore crypto and NFTs was by sharing my journey and walking the walk together. I guested on Clubhouse panels, wrote essays detailing my learnings, answered interviews by major media like *Complex*, guested on mainstream podcasts like Kevin Smith's *SModcast* and NPR, and tweeted my opinions regularly. Although crypto Twitter had loud crypto influencers and sophisticated thought leaders alike, there were few personalities who could package the dense information in a digestible format for the layman. Since I was one of those neophytes myself, it was easier

---

ily the subject matter you often associate with Big Tech. Meanwhile, this vocabulary is the bedrock of streetwear, something we know and practice well.

for me to parse the data for the everyday collector more interested in sneakers than Solana.

For the last several years, Instagram has been the default social media across the board. More specifically, young people use Snapchat to text, their grandparents share fake news on Facebook, and TikTok has taken the internet by storm. But when it comes to crypto, Twitter (and in the past, Clubhouse) is the preeminent social platform because the engagement and activity are not products of posting cute selfies or going viral with a dance challenge. NFTs are very much a nascent, abstruse phenomenon stoked by collaboration, conversation, and creation. To be into NFTs means sharing your thoughts and playing a part in their origin stories. For every JPEG you buy and sell on Ethereum, for every metaverse you test out, for every wallet that gets drained, you're writing history. That's why I say it's culture before crypto. It's cliché and corny, but NFTs truly are about the community . . . and by the community.

Has there ever been a revolutionary technology that's been discovered, explored, and forged while it's still being built? Furthermore, one that's being assessed by a largely anonymous, decentralized community around the world, each tendering unlettered opinions as to how to build the boat in real time? The discussion and pontification are happening so fast on Twitter, that WhatsApp groups and Telegram chats act as breakaway rooms to ideate even more efficiently on a micro scale.

The positive results are that Web3 innovation is moving at breakneck speed. You're seeing experiments rise and fall in a fortnight and good ideas rapidly evolving, raising money, and turning into formidable companies. There's little room to entertain silly blockchain use cases, so the wheat's separating from the chaff with haste. The downside is that the entire space is buckling under the weight of impatience, short attention spans, unrealistic expectations, and little forgiveness. NFTs' tallest impediment is that the conversation is fast outpacing the infrastructure. People are in such a hysteric rush to mint projects and make money, they are exposing themselves to thieves and swindlers—"rugpullers" or "ruggers"—who are quick to take advantage of the sloppy and greedy. The metaverse topic is important and worth the investment. But the froth around start-up metaverses like Sandbox and Decentraland foamed up and flattened out within a season. People are so nearsighted, they aren't willing to stick around five to ten years to see Facebook's Meta materialize. And yet, that's exactly how long it's taken for most of your favorite parts of the internet to come to fruition. Although this makes no sense, if people had visibility on early social apps during their development process and could find a way to theorize about and critique the tech together, there's no way we would've gotten this far. The process would have taken too long, consumers would have lost faith, and the cancel-happy critics would have resisted any iota of disruptive progress to preserve their present comfort.

When it comes to the cynics and haters—the "FUD" (fear, uncertainty, doubt)—that's one aspect of Web3 that I had to accept and swallow early on. The meme has been in play since the beginning of time: People are afraid of what they don't understand. And that fear can unwind into contempt, confusion, or absolute loathing. In the nine-

NFTS ARE A SCAM

teenth century, a band of English textile workers fought back against machines that threatened to take their jobs, earmarking the beginnings of the humans versus robots war. Today, a "Luddite" is someone who is opposed to new technology and automated progression because of the worry of human replacement.

This is hard to picture in the land of TikTok and StockX, but when The Hundreds came onto the streetwear scene in the early 2000s, we were mocked and blocked for not only having a website, but having one that featured e-commerce and a regularly updated blog. The gatekeepers had very specific notions of streetwear as a private club, tucked away from the lurking eyes of the internet. In their minds, the idea that we'd transparentize the brand by exposing the daily goings-on, from whom we were hanging out with to projects we were working on, also directly contradicted streetwear's secretive nature.

But as time would tell, they weren't opposed to our philosophy and practices as much as they were bewildered by the tech and its paradigm shift. Most of the veterans were accustomed to being cosigned by centralized, gatekept print magazines like *Mass Appeal* and *Paper*, not digital blogs by foreign fanboys like Hypebeast and SlamXhype. Brands were used to governing distribution channels like specific retail partners or flagship stores. E-commerce and eBay made the product more accessible, especially to those who were geographically distanced from the cool boutiques. Social media compressed the distance between brand and consumer. Now there was a direct mode of communication—all mystery and hierarchy were flattened. Traditional streetwear is obsessed with guarding their brands. New technologies threaten control and force powerful people to not only face that they're being rendered obsolete, but to leave their comfort zones. They don't like that.

Over time, streetwear would reluctantly adopt the blog thing, then the social media thing. They didn't have much of a choice but to open their e-commerce doors since other people were buying and selling their product on resale sites anyway. Supreme even took the initiative to launch their own app. For the most part, however, streetwear tends to rest on the back-half of tech innovation, waiting for others to imagine, execute, and normalize it before they hold hands and make the jump in unison. I can also say the same for crypto and NFTs. Most brands and personalities in streetwear are still watching from the wings while Verbal from AMBUSH, Jeff Staple, and of course myself and The Hundreds, persist. Hiroshi Fujiwara, the godfather of streetwear, launched a Solana project in 2021. A Bathing Ape has their (B)APETAVERSE. As for the rest of them, there is no doubt in my mind that the culture will catch on as more influencers plant their flags (this will also most likely come by way of Nike's foray into Web3).

I can't really blame people for hating NFTs. For one, most people who attack them aren't properly educated on the breadth of what they are and what they can accomplish. Instead, the media likes to frame NFTs exclusively as million-dollar monkey JPEGs that you trade down to the freshest idiot. That's fair. Even the long-game builders and engineers have partaken in the Web3 casino. When I was in college, I was paying my rent by flipping domain names. Just because some art can be grossly resold for millions of dollars doesn't discount the importance and value of art as a whole. Entire civilizations and cultures have been discovered and settled by opportunistic capitalism. Oil. Diamonds. Automobiles. The Gold Rush filled in Northern California (as did the dot-com boom). Between 1846 and 1852, San Francisco went from two hundred residents to thirty-six thousand. I'm sure these people foresaw the vast potential of populating the verdant land around the Bay Area, but what initially attracted them there was the fast-tracked possibility of getting rich quick.

Leading up to Adam Bomb Squad's release, it was important for us to educate and onboard our endemic The Hundreds community to NFTs. Seeing how fast and finicky crypto collectors moved, we wanted the cultural backbone of our collection to be shouldered by people who had a thorough understanding of how deliberately and thoughtfully we build brands. The Hundreds had survived decades of vicious trend cycles and streetwear droughts by sidestepping low hanging fruit and reinvesting in longevity. Over the years, we watched countless streetwear peers take the glittering paycheck from low-quality retailers or sign deals with bad investors. Although they enjoyed sudden success, their growth was rarely sustainable as the infrastructure and brand cache never had the time to organically build and defend itself against mainstream demand.

In the summer of 2021, we observed other NFT projects like Bored Apes starting up like the Humanoids, Lazy Lions, and World of Women. Although most collections had the support of a core community on their Discord and Twitter, there were also a legion of NFT traders punching in and out of projects for a quick flip. In fact, many of the founders seemed they were in for the pump-and-dump themselves. As much as I wanted to decry those who shirked brand loyalty and were merely in it for the money, I also knew that the flippers keep the energy churning for the ecosystem and attract newcomers. Everyone plays a part.*

The biggest mistake that celebrities, influencers, and brands make when entering the NFT space is that they approach the tech like a ploy instead of a culture. A marketing gimmick or trend requires low effort and can be easily adopted by anyone. It's a viral TikTok challenge, a pop-up shop, influencer marketing, an experiential activation, or a specifically colored hoodie. To some of these people, NFTs are the new podcast. The proper way to understand NFTs, however, is that they aren't the talk show. They're what you talk about on that show. NFTs are presented as cartoon pictures, but what they represent is a movement, philosophy, and a way of life. Crypto is as much of a statement about finance and government as it is a fungible currency. Most people don't identify with marketing schemes, but NFTs encapsulate a person's taste in art, stance on wealth disparity, and social circle.

Now, imagine a pop musician or A-list actor waltzing into the space, announcing that they are selling ten thousand NFTs without being additive to the culture. You can see why most of these characters, no matter how popular

* In sneaker collecting, there's Nike, there are the authorized retailers and secondhand stores, there's the sneakerhead who's "for the culture," and then there's the reseller.

and successful in other facets of their career, are NGMI ("not gonna make it") in crypto. Their endemic fans are confused without context; this certainly comes off as a cash-grab. They're also ill-equipped to navigate crypto because nobody guided them in. The deep crypto crowd is also skeptical and sus of this surprise enthusiasm for NFTs. It's a fail on all sides.

For the year before we dropped Adam Bomb Squad, we lived crypto, breathed NFTs, and invested in friendships with people from around the world who were down for the cause. To show our commitment and belief in the space, we were the first streetwear brand to officially collaborate with many of the NFT trailblazers like Larva Labs' CryptoPunks, Bored Ape Yacht Club, Deadfellaz, Amber Vittoria, Drift, and Cool Cats. This not only introduced our existing following to a new category of creative brands and artists, we also welcomed their audiences to The Hundreds as well.*

As we were prepping both The Hundreds' and NFT communities for Adam Bomb Squad throughout the summer of 2021, we assembled tens of thousands of permutations of Adam, Madam, and Badam Bombs. As we got closer to the deadline, we put every designer in the building on the project to dig up original illustrations of bombs from our archives, oversee quality assurance, and edit the best-looking bombs into the final cut. The bombs were either graphics we had designed in the past

* Instead of leaning on traditional advertising or marketing campaigns, much of our brand awareness over the years has come by way of cross-pollinating audiences through collaborations. It's an organic means of growing the brand's base, by highlighting the commonalities between the parties.

as T-shirts or "Simples" and "Pures." Simple bombs were one-color. Pure bombs were a unique combination of colors, because so much of streetwear design is characterized by appealing colorways. There was also an assortment of bombs that were cut from prior clothing collections or were never even finalized out of the drafts folder. We resurrected many of those bombs for Adam Bomb Squad as well.

To make each bomb unique, we layered them on a distinct background that was pulled from The Hundreds' library. These were either solid base colors (that directly corresponded with T-shirt Pantones that we use in our apparel collections) or custom patterns that we've employed at some point in our cut-and-sew. Examples of ABS backgrounds ranged from a spectrum of The Hundreds–specific camouflages, yarn-dyed stripes, Hawaiian prints, repeating patterns like roses and cherries, and plaids. One of my favorite backgrounds is Faded Black, which is the shade between an opaque black and a dusty dark gray that a black T-shirt falls into over multiple washes.

Although every bomb was tied to unique art and coded with a specific stamp on the Ethereum blockchain, there needed to be even more nuanced distinction among NFTs in the Adam Bomb Squad. There are Sticker bombs that feature a red, blue, or green sticker in the top right corner.* There's a series of bombs called Double Trouble where identical twins are differentiated only by a small denotation in the corner. Error Terror bombs are a tribute to a 2021 Topps baseball card campaign I collaborated

---

* RGB is one of The Hundreds' color schemes, a reference to our background in web design as a digital brand in the mid-2000s.

NFTS ARE A SCAM

on while building Adam Bomb Squad. These NFTs feature glitches and mistakes that happened in the design or minting process.

While most of the bombs shared traits in tribes (all the bombs with hairstyles, bombs on paisley backgrounds, bombs that look like skulls), there are a select number of bombs that had only a few companions in the entire collection. For instance, there are only five Reverse Adams in Adam Bomb Squad—these are Adam Bombs that are facing to the left instead of the usual right. Of all the Adam Bombs wearing fedora hats, only two are colored. And then there is the Black Adam, the rarest bomb of all and positioned as number one on ranking sites. Black Adam is the closest Adam Bomb to the original design in the trademark red, black, yellow, and white colors on a classic black background. There is only one like it and the whale collector 888 bought it from the original owner for hundreds of thousands of dollars.*

On August 27, 2021, I put on an Adam Bomb T-shirt and snapped a selfie on my front lawn as I stepped out into the sun. It was Adam Bomb Day and we were set to release twenty-five thousand Adam Bomb Squad NFTs into the wild. By the time I returned to my door that evening, I knew my life would be forever changed. It's not that I ex-

---

* The backstory behind Black Adam runs even deeper in The Hundreds' lore. Our rarest T-shirt—the Black Adam T-shirt—has never been offered for sale and can only be gifted by either Ben or I personally. There've probably been no more than seventy of these distributed around the world.

pected the money to impact my circumstances (in fact, considering Ben and I had eased off clothing production because we'd dedicated our entire year to developing digital art, we'd probably close out 2021 about even for the company). It's that we were about to proclaim to the world that we were actively in the NFT space with a credible project. Without any skin in the game, I'd been an NFT influencer at worst, a meddling pundit at best. Now, I would have a legitimate basis upon which to speak on the matter.

Twenty-five thousand NFTs was a lot. And these were edited down from a pool of double that number. Each bomb had been scrutinized, centered, and tuned, and approved by Ben, myself, and the team. Every NFT was there for a reason. In those days, the standard count for collections hovered around ten thousand NFTs. Larva Labs set this precedent back in 2017 with CryptoPunks and although I'm sure they had a specific reason as to why they designated this amount, the 2021 projects adopted ten thousand arbitrarily. Theoretically, the more scarce the supply, the higher the individual value. A popular anime-themed project called 0N1 Force had minted out the week prior to Adam Bomb Squad. With only 7,777 NFTs in circulation, their reselling price on the secondary market was substantial. But more NFTs could also mean more holders, leading to a greater chance of marketing notoriety and mainstream proliferation.

With The Hundreds, we never sought to devise an exclusive, inaccessible brand. Many of the designers we admired were so obscure and unattainable, that they were more art projects and snobbish statements than scalable fashion labels. Meanwhile, our brand is meant for anyone who is willing to walk the journey with us. When we started, our generation of brands marked a turning point in streetwear where we transitioned from exclusive to inclusive and flagship to wholesale. While prior streetwear generations protected the secret, we believed that the secret was so good that we wanted to share it with as many people as possible.

The most popular NFT collections were adhering to this arbitrary ten thousand number, but Ben wondered why couldn't there be one that was fifteen thousand? Twenty thousand? One of our devs, Dylan Reed a.k.a. Nervous, pontificated, "Somebody is gonna break through that one-hundred-thousand-unit barrier one day. Might as well be you guys!" With more people coming into the space and new projects minting every day, it'd be silly to be handcuffed to this quantity (set in 2017) in the years to come. Having said that, in 2021, the market still wasn't prepared to swallow a number that big. We finally compromised on twenty-five thousand bombs at 0.1 ETH each. Ben was convinced we'd sell out, but I was dubious. At the time, this was two and a half times the size of a typical NFT project, and it was important to sell as many bombs—as quickly as possible—to sustain a high value on the secondary marketplace.

Most novices don't grasp this aspect of NFTs. A win in this marketplace isn't an isolated target. Selling out of a collection isn't the goal; it's merely the beginning. To be honest, it's expected. Instead, a project's merit is assessed in perpetuity, and hinges on how high its NFTs are trading for above the initial mint price on auction sites. Participants of the resale economy—sneaker flippers, art buyers, and card collectors, for example—are steeped in this game, which is set to be worth $64 billion by 2024. A good product sells out. But an exceptional product commands a greater price tag at auction. That means that the demand is so high for the product, and there's such a scarce supply, that people are willing to pay a premium to the owner to best the rest. This then turns the feedback loop and amplifies the allure of the product to the next generation of bidders. It's like entering the highest bid for a dream house in a good neighborhood. There is a set and finite supply of homes near the desired elementary school. As the population grows in the region, the value of that investment rises as it becomes more precious.

To prevent an excess supply, we came up with a plan to "blow up" any bombs that didn't sell within five days. So, if only five thousand bombs sold, that would be our new capped amount by week's end. We'd then play a fitting animation on the site detonating the other twenty thousand stragglers. I wasn't even sure we could sell five thousand bombs, although there were some reasons to be confident. The NFT community is rabid and moves about virally. After we teased a forthcoming NFT collection from The Hundreds, our Discord was crawling with tens of thousands of new subscribers, hunting for the inside scoop. Gary Vaynerchuk's ONE37pm website shouted us out in their daily recap the day before our release, and the Bored Ape community was tracking us after our collaboration had blown out the week before the ABS mint. I'd also amassed a new crypto Twitter audience, surpassing one hundred thousand followers on my personal account. And The Hundreds had made a name for itself in the NFT world, tracing all the way back to our CryptoPunks hat at the start of the year. Above all, we were unlike any other NFT project in that we had a built-in community that had supported us for years. Other NFT brands were starting from scratch. We were standing atop a legacy with a global network of fans and friends.

That was the one truth that made me most bullish about Adam Bomb Squad among a sea of competitors: longest history, longest future. NFT projects were essentially raising capital to start assembling a veritable brand. We were decades ahead of them and had proven ourselves with a time-tested business. This reassured those looking to back trustworthy founders—not just because we've thrived and survived in feast and famine, but because we are public figures (doxed). Crypto's nature is to be anonymous, so most NFT projects are founded and promoted by the nameless and faceless. This doesn't always mean that these characters are shadowy and ill-willed, but it does feel better knowing that if you're supporting a brand, there is real-world accountability in case things go south.

It was a double-edged sword, however. The very fact that our reputation preceded us meant that people had preconceived notions of what we were, for better and for worse. The Hundreds was a reputable fashion brand that was digitally native and had capitalized on blogging, media, and e-commerce since the early 2000s. Yet we were not regarded as a proven tech company. We've always been arts-focused and culture-forward, but don't have access to solidity engineers and virtual reality designers. Perhaps NFT collectors would feel insecure about that blind spot.

Also, many in the Web3 space pigeonholed us as a Web2 company because that's all they'd ever known. The odds were probably higher that if they had ETH to spare, they'd pledge it to the mysterious and novel instead. Rather than commit to the familiar and predictable, speculators tend to have a wandering eye for the new girl. It's funny how people would rather place their bets on an unknown— based off colorful promises and hope—than invest in what's real right in front of them. That speaks to both the romantic and greedy side of Web3. The ravenous appetite for newness. The romantic quest for the next big thing. And we saw it all around us in this stage of NFTs: people pouring crypto into anon teams riding in on dazzling road maps of thoughts and prayers. It was reckless and foolish, but it was also stunning to watch unfold. Strangers from around the world, risking it all because of the promise of betterment on the other side. This was incredible conviction in not just the technology, but in the people who comprised the community.*

We hadn't settled on an exact time to drop Adam Bomb Squad that warm August morning. These days, there are hard dates and times structured around NFT releases, along with marketing calendars, membership passes, allow-list presales, and other formulas to ensure a speedy sell-out into a strong floor price on the secondary market.

* A year later, much of that rosiness would fade, but for those who continued to build in a sagging bear market that passionate affair sustains.

In the summer of 2021, there were fewer specifics set in stone, meaning looser expectations, encouraging creativity and flexibility in how collections were distributed. We had collectively agreed that we'd give our friends and existing core The Hundreds community a tiny bit of a head start before the general public could dive into the sale. Again, there were twenty-five thousand bombs. Perhaps we'd let it run for an hour for the early birds before dropping the gate.

There were two devs on our project, Allen and Dylan, calling in from different cities. The Adam Bomb Squad team spanned the country in three equidistant dots, capping both coasts and the middle of the United States. Meanwhile, in our L.A. offices, our digital brand manager Sandy, summer intern Jack, and I were standing around Ben and his computer as we prepared to deploy the bombs.

"Ready?" Dylan asked over speakerphone.

Ben made that anxious emoji face, baring his teeth. The rest of us shrugged and nodded in concurrence. "Let's GOOOO," he roared. Dylan flipped the switch on his side, unlocking the minting webpage. Over Zoom, Allen was monitoring what was happening on the back end. Since all blockchain activity is public, he could see which wallet addresses were buying and how many. We hadn't capped a limit on bombs, assuming that at $330 a pop (not including gas fees to transact on the Ethereum blockchain), most collectors wouldn't go too far overboard.

Another thing projects didn't think too much about back then was locking in free and clear release dates. Countless NFT collections were minting every day and overwhelming the Ethereum blockchain with activity. Gas fees (the cost of computing energy required to process transactions) were thus skyrocketing, sometimes becoming as much as—if not more than—the price of the NFTs themselves.* As a result, the ETH miners (the real-life human beings who are solving cryptographic puzzles to add the blocks to the blockchain) were arguably the most prosperous wing of the ecosystem back then. They even earned gas fees whether the transaction succeeded or not!†

Not only were we unprepared for the gas wars, we were also unaware that a very popular project—Art Blocks—was minting out their collection at the very same time as us. The Ethereum blockchain was getting hammered from all sides.‡ Yet it didn't seem to matter as our bombs were dispersing into the universe like confetti tossed into the wind.

---

* On the last day of April 2022, the Bored Ape Yacht Club's parent company, Yuga Labs, debuted their long-awaited metaverse. Otherside promptly became the largest NFT mint to date at fifty-five thousand plots of land. Each NFT cost a whopping $5,800 to mint, meaning Yuga made around $320 million in less than four hours. What was even more shocking, however, was that the ETH miners made half as much as Yuga. Buyers were pounding on the Ether network so hard that average gas fees around the NFT marketplace surged to $500. Consequently, other NFT floors drained for two reasons: (1) People paused on trading NFTs that weren't Yuga or Otherside-related. (2) Even worse, collectors started liquidating their NFTs to pay for Yuga's digital land. Especially once they slammed into prohibitively expensive gas estimates that were one hundred to two hundred times the normal fees.

Some paid up to $6,500 in gas charges on top of buying the NFT. One holder burned $44,000 in fees for two Otherside NFTs (while critics blamed Yuga for a bad contract, Ethereum cofounder Vitalik Buterin tweeted that optimizing the smart contract wouldn't have ameliorated the situation. Yuga Labs semiapologized anyway). Overall, Otherside buyers spent over $176 million just in gas fees to the miners. This includes the $4.4 million lost in fees over fifteen thousand failed transactions (which Yuga eventually refunded).

† In the future, this will become more of a moot issue because in September 2022, the Ethereum blockchain merged from a proof-of-work system to proof-of-stake. I'm not going to get into it, but the groundwork has now been laid for infrastructure for cheaper fees and lesser congestion.

‡ In fact, according to OpenSea statistics, August 27 was the date of peak activity in their marketplace for 2021. After that day, NFT trading volume steadily declined until the surge returned in the new year.

We couldn't believe our eyes. Whales, influencers, close friends and family, and, of course, The Hundreds community were partaking in the feast. My WhatsApp and Telegram group chats were exploding like fireworks, half with congratulations, the other half with gripes about clogged networks and gas fees. In less than forty minutes, the twenty-five thousandth Adam Bomb Squad NFT was claimed (and the first rumblings of online grief from those who missed out welled up). The room sat silent but was rife with electricity.

We'd spent the entire year working tirelessly on our first major NFT collection. Most projects are completed in a fraction of the time. The Yuga Labs guys told us Bored Apes was just a couple of months from idea to execution. But our project was built differently, infused with annals of storytelling and gamification and history. Adam Bomb Squad's art wasn't randomized or algorithmically manufactured. Each bomb was forged with ample—and intentional—data points. Every Adam, Badam, and Madam had passed through our team's hands multiple times. Plus, there were two to three times more NFTs in our collection compared to the average project. That meant at least two to three times the labor, care, and consideration.

Sandy ran down the hall to her cubicle and returned with a bottle of champagne.

"Let's have a sip!" She grinned as she unwrapped a party pack of plastic flutes.

Ben grimaced. "I hate celebrating too soon."

"Come on . . . We should remember this!"

The four of us—Ben, myself, Sandy, and our intern Jack—threw out a wary "Cheers!" looked each other in the eyes, and tilted the flimsy glasses back. The warm champagne tingled in the back of our throats and faded fast. My mouth ran dry as I took the brief pause to appreciate all that we had accomplished. We'd been through so many ups and downs in the fashion business, that I knew that nothing lasts forever. In fact, wins and losses are hard to differentiate from each other with the passage of time and evolution of life. But I've also been around long enough to know that when the sun steals through the clouds, you roll out that picnic blanket and drink in the light. Careers can be hard and riddled with pain. It's important to know when to stop and count your blessings, especially if the road to that rest stop was uphill and treacherous.

In the early afternoon, my son texted me from his school bus.

"Dad. Did the Adam Bomb Squad do good?"

"It sold out!"

"Wait all of it"

"Yes all of it!"

"That's what you wanted right. OMG"

"It's what we wanted. We are very happy. Are you?"

"Yes. Wow. Is everyone happy"

"Yes they are. I love you."

"I love you."

I screen-grabbed that interaction and have it saved on my phone. I read it over as the first portentous storm clouds rolled in overnight into our Discord. I read it again as the hopium high wore off and segments of the community turned against me in my Twitter replies. And over the year, as the crypto market crashed and NFTs slipped off the edge, I opened that conversation to remind myself, "It's what we wanted."

"What now?" I asked aloud, as I flipped the champagne flute into the wastebasket.

The next steps were clear. We had to deliver the art to the holders. Upon mint, most NFT collections distribute a generic placeholder image that is later unwrapped to expose the underlying unique art. You're collecting blindly the way that you would buy a Pokémon pack or a box of football cards. Bluntly, it's closer to gambling on a chance casino game. "Wen reveal" is a customary chant across Discord forums the moment a project's NFTs mint through. "When are you going to show us what we got!?" It's a fleeting stage of euphoria in which thousands of buyers all believe their chocolate bar is hiding Willy Wonka's golden ticket. It's that pregnant pause before the lottery numbers are called and every player is daydreaming of a better life. And of course, it's the last time that everyone collectively views the project in a positive light.

Because the reality is that most people will not hold something special, comparatively speaking. Sure, the art will have inherent value and purpose. But the market self-curates in a way to demarcate some NFTs as better than others, even if on a ruthlessly arbitrary basis (not unlike a freshman class shuffling out who the popular kids are). As soon as the cards are turned, everyone's in a mad rush to trade, dump, and rummage for information about how valuable (a.k.a. expensive) their NFT is. You can look directly into the NFT's metadata, which is engraved on the blockchain. Every collectible is stacked with traits, which are purposefully choreographed or randomly distributed in a spectrum of rarities.

"How many NFTs have the 3D glasses attribute?"

"Is it rare that mine is gold?"

"Why is mine facing the wrong way?"

There are also rarity ranking websites that look past the art and assess the metadata alone, appraising the leading collections by the auditor's own subjective standards. Upon reveals, flippers scrutinize these hierarchies to tell them which NFTs are more desirable. At this stage in the process, there is little—if any—consideration for the art or designs in determining happiness with the product. The WAGMI ("We're All Gonna Make It!") stage of the NFT life cycle has closed as holders' satisfaction now depends on what the collectible can fetch at auction. You know how social media has tabulated our self-worth into follower counts and numbers of likes? NFTs are judged by a simple score known as the FP, or "floor price." What is the absolute base amount of money somebody would pay for the least coveted NFT in this entire collection? That number now exclusively dictates an NFT project's entire worth.

Yes, I agree with you. It's a stupid and cannibalistic system. It debases the art and makes NFTs solely about the cheapest trading value. It forces FUD and buyer's remorse for most of the people who bought in. And it not only invites but promotes an exploitative, opportunistic hustle versus a collaborative, cooperative community. The game turns into buying in low and getting out high before the entire model falls apart, which essentially means that you're passing the buck to a more unfortunate soul. You don't want to be the last one at the party, left holding the bag. This is the part where critics and haters feel justified in classifying NFTs as pyramid or Ponzi schemes.

The system, however, is remarkably efficient in reducing NFTs to financial instruments and transactional assets. It gets all that frivolous "creative" stuff out of the way and makes a lot of people a lot of money very fast, drawing attention and energy to a new medium in an otherwise stagnant pandemic climate. But it's not only hostile to a burgeoning industry trying to spread its roots, it's unsustainable and can be corrosive to an art form. I've seen this countless times in streetwear and sneakers. Whenever street fashion becomes about the cash over the culture, it goes off the rails. When streetwear drops are about the profitability over the product design, its consumers don't look at each other as friends with shared interests. Instead, they see each other as competitors (at best) and enemies (at worst). The consequences can be physically violent (flare-ups in line), but also spiritually calamitous. Once you lose the balance between art and commerce, you can lose the plot.

It wasn't long ago when NFTs were anchored and led by the art. At the end of 2020, the crypto headlines were dedicated to esteemed artists like Pak. Within a year, however, the art, innovation, and culture of NFTs were driven by ETH. This was due to crypto's meteoric trajectory at the time. It was also due to the sensational Bored Ape effect on NFT sales. It was futile to try to correct this aberration on our own, but we believed we could use the Adam Bomb Squad reveal to make a statement about art and reboot the bloodthirsty NFT mindset.

So we tried something different. When we refreshed the IPFS (the network hosting the NFT data) and revealed everyone's NFTs, they were published with zero metadata! That meant that people could see their art, but there was no information about their NFTs' traits attached to the file, no statistical data to measure it against others, and no way of quantifying the NFT outside of mere aesthetics. We were bombarded with questions.

"Can you tell me about my bomb?"

"Mine looks similar to my friend's, but the eyes are hollowed out. Is this a mistake?"

"What is the significance of red, green, and blue stickers?"

Basically, they were asking, "Is mine expensive?"

We couldn't answer that question, however, because we weren't the ones to decide that—they were. This was intended to be a retrospective of Adam Bomb's history, so we encouraged people to do their research and come up with their own conclusions. Years of storytelling were embedded into The Hundreds' blog, social copy, and other editorial. We urged our holders to establish their own relationship with their bombs, distinct from how a ranking website or floor price might influence their perception of the NFT.

We promised the community that the metadata would

eventually arrive, but even when it did, it would be virtually useless in defining rarities if plugged into a machine. The message was that art isn't special because of some third-party number crunching. Art becomes meaningful when it personally moves the observer. Of course, money and financial value energize the art ecosystem, but we wanted to give our project time to take shape organically before it was repackaged as a dispensable product. Streetwear had decades of organic run-up before online secondary sales prioritized the monetary value over design and story. This legacy gave the brands and designers in street fashion time for deep roots to take hold. Therefore, even with trends now driven by price tags and resale prices, streetwear's longstanding traditions, rituals, and code infuse humanness to the equation.

At first, many in the Adam Bomb Squad were livid—especially those who had entered the community with the specific purpose of making fast ETH and exiting with haste. This not only foiled their plans for a quick departure, but they were now tasked with homework if they wanted to evaluate their collectible. That meant logging on to our Discord and engaging with core The Hundreds supporters who were versed in the brand's history. I spent countless hours a day in that room in those first couple of months, answering as many questions about the art as possible for those who were curious. Collectors were also forced to compare notes with other ABS members who were similarly hunting for insight. Many did the deep dive and examined all twenty-five thousand bombs in the NFT collection. A few people made their own Google spreadsheets of bombs and traits to diagnose differences.

Others took to reading my book or researching thousands of blog archives to get an advantage.

If you were here to flip, we didn't make it easy. Many of the impatient traders called it quits and cashed in their chips, setting out on the secondary NFT marketplace OpenSea to score on NFTs that were more straightforward and formulaic. As time went on, however, the ones who stuck around Adam Bomb Squad started talking about their NFTs differently. Some started to grasp how specialness is not always defined by data. Value is subjectively interpreted. It can be shaped by emotions, nostalgia, influencer cosigns, larger market trends, and social climate. As had been proven in early projects like CryptoPunks, just because a trait was scarce (like "buckteeth"), it didn't make it popular or more valuable in the marketplace. Vice versa, a more prevalent trait like a purple hat could become a hot commodity, especially if a famous mouthpiece like Gary Vee vouched for it.

Looking back, I think the point I was really trying to prove was that Adam Bomb Squad wasn't going to be held prisoner to someone else's data analysis. If The Hundreds had been run through the same algorithms in its early days, we wouldn't have stood a chance. No computer could quantify our focus, drive, and heart. And I'd be damned if robots would govern the outcome of our NFT project. Adam Bomb Squad's fate wasn't even in my hands or The Hundreds'. It was up to the community to decide how big and how far this could go. It would be a true test of decentralized brand-building.

We weren't trying to irritate the traders, but they were quick to turn against us. We were amazed at how urgently NFT people wanted their metadata, but even more stunned at how fast they were prepared to burn the place down if they couldn't spin a hot flip. One day, a disenchanted holder in my Discord told me that nobody had faith in me and that I had failed them. I was speechless. Of course, after decades in streetwear, I'm accustomed and numb to hate and trolling, even from our own customers. This felt different, however. Like the calls were coming from inside the house. One of the most painful moments was hearing through the grapevine that childhood friends were bad-mouthing us behind our back. It was one thing for outsiders to rail against the project or criticize top-down decisions. It was another for close confidants to text us how we were doing out of friendly concern, while commiserating with strangers in private Telegram chats to talk shit on us.

To add fuel to the fire, it didn't help that we decided to draw out the metadata reveal just a couple of weeks longer so that I could write more thorough stories in the metadata. Most projects weren't backed by exhaustive narratives because they had appeared out of thin air. Our metadata, however, granted us parchment to elaborate on the design choices and historical purpose behind every Adam, Badam, and Madam Bomb NFT. After we revealed the art and I was constantly getting solicited for explanations behind the NFTs, I realized that we had missed a valuable opportunity in articulating the holistic Adam Bomb universe. So for two weeks straight, we reopened the metadata and I went in and detailed the origins and identity of all twenty-five thousand NFTs.

I did it because we weren't building a project for the

next twelve months. We were in this for the long haul and the more information I could pack into the trunk, the further our journey could run. The Hundreds has been around for twenty years and most days, it feels like we're only just getting started. Our background is in building thoughtful brands with longevity. It took The Hundreds three years just to turn a profit. Meanwhile, most NFT collectors—and even the NFT founders and artists—aren't even planning for three months out. Sometimes, if not most of the time, crypto constituents behave like it's all going to disappear in a heartbeat. NFT traders exhibit this type of attitude in the way that they pump and dump projects with expediency. The scammier NFT project founders are even worse, anonymously releasing projects and disappearing into the night with a greasy bag of ETH in tow. This is probably one of crypto's most vulnerable frailties: behind closed doors, not many hold the steadfast conviction they loudly profess. At the end of the day, many of these diehards will flee to fiat currency at the first sign of instability.

The morning after the sale, I was loading my surfboard into the back of my truck when I ran into Matt Colon.*

"Congrats on Adam Bomb Squad. How're you doing?"

"Yeah, not bad. But, man, I didn't expect so many demands."

---

* You remember my neighbor Matt Colon—who manages not only 3LAU but NFTs' biggest celebrity, Steve Aoki.

Matt laughed. "Everybody thinks that launching the NFT project is when the work ends. But that's where the work begins!"

From that day forward, my life has never been the same. What followed was the most thrilling and the hardest twelve months of my entire career. One of the many things that I underestimated was the weight of the community. While most projects have about three to five thousand unique wallets holding their NFTs, we've carried around 8,500. Although unique individuals can technically have multiple wallets, it's probably not too far off the mark to assume we have over eight thousand people in our community. That's 8,500 different opinions; 8,500 new customers we didn't have before with 8,500 new complaints. One of the first benefits we promised in minting an ABS NFT was a free T-shirt. It's not the cost of the goods and production that had us shook. It was the labor and time to produce 8,500 T-shirts, mail them out individually, and manage the customer service on the back end.

Eight thousand five hundred sets of expectations. Although most everyone in the community has been content, quiet, or both, it takes only a few vocal FUDders to color the vibes of an entire project. For many, the floor price was never high enough—especially in comparison to some of the blue-chip collections like Cool Cats and Bored Apes. There was suddenly a lot of speculation and theorizing as to why the value of our NFTs wasn't exploding the way Doodles or Creature World did. One hypothesis was that there was a surplus at twenty-five thousand NFTs. "There are too many bombs!" people grumbled (this didn't seem like a problem before they bought into the project). "Burn them!" They wanted us to incentivize people who held multiple bombs to send gratuitous ABS NFTs to a null address, which meant they'd effectively be lost in the ether (not Ethereum) and shrink the overall supply. We disagreed. Again, Ben and I were building a collection to play for the rest of our lives. If the world eventually adopted Web3 the way we anticipated, then twenty-five thousand wouldn't be enough! Plus, there was scant difference between the average ten thousand NFTs and twenty-five thousand in the grand scheme. Especially if millions—and then billions—of people would onboard to NFTs over time. Not long after we minted out, more NFT collections broke through the ten thousand supply count. RTFKT's CloneX has twenty thousand items. VeeFriends 2 has over fifty-four thousand NFTs in its collection. And there are one hundred thousand Yuga Labs' Otherdeeds.

Some in the community wanted me to be a more bellicose salesperson and shill the bombs at every opportunity. I've never been a salesman; I believe in letting the work speak for itself. I also know that I can peddle some NFTs here and there, but in the end, that thirstiness would compromise our brand integrity and hurt us in the long run. There were even the occasional requests for the founders to walk onto the secondary market and sweep the floor. Basically, they wanted us to spend the ETH we'd earned to go and buy bombs back from the community. In good conscience, we couldn't do it. Beyond a moral gesture, however, we knew that floor-sweeping wasn't gonna last. In fact, phony insider manipulation like that can backfire by temporarily juicing the market. If there isn't anything organic to back that energy up, there's a long fall from grace on the other side. You can wind up in a much worse spot than you were in before—except this time, you've wasted your funds.

Utility. When we had embarked on developing this project over half a year before, NFT collections weren't expected to provide any usefulness beyond delivering unique art. By the time we deployed the bombs, largely because of the Bored Apes' marketing around utility, every project was suddenly expected to come equipped with a greater purpose than aesthetic enjoyment. Thankfully, because The Hundreds was a running machine, we had a lot to offer. One of our first bits of utility was offering free food for all Adam Bomb Squad holders who attended our festival, Family Style. But then one person unspooled about how he had spent thousands of dollars on our NFTs and all he got in return was a free chicken sandwich? So I started doing "Chicken Sandwich" updates, which were code for all the utility we had given the community. We got them on the allow list for hot NFT projects. We delivered free Xboxes to specific holders of video-game-themed Adam Bombs. All ABS holders get 10 percent off at The Hundreds flagship store. If you held a Joshua Vides collaboration bomb, we sent you a $600 collaborative rug. Anyone with an Error Terror NFT got a baseball card from my Topps artist series.

My white paper, "The Street Does Not Really Exist"— the Jerry Maguire manifesto for Adam Bomb Squad—was based on this notion of resetting the brand-consumer relationship. The pie-in-the-sky dream was that if the bomb on your ABS NFT wound up on a piece of The

Hundreds apparel, you would earn royalties from those sales. In theory, this should not only inspire people to own an Adam Bomb Squad NFT but to promote their bomb to raise awareness for The Hundreds and generate more sales. Now, both the brand and the community are aligned as far as goals and purpose.

By the end of 2021, however, the federal government was hovering more fiercely around crypto.* So, we offered holders store credit and gift cards. Then, by the summer of 2022, we introduced L(ABS), whereby you could buy customized The Hundreds merchandise from our online shop featuring your Adam Bomb Squad NFT instead of traditional The Hundreds branding. This made for hyper-limited, one-of-one goods for the fan.

Adam Bomb Squad was recognized by press like *Ad Age* and Hypebeast for being a leader in bridging Web2 brands to Web3. There are still very few existing brands that adopt NFTs, and only a handful that achieve any meaningful success in crypto. While larger corporations like Starbucks, Universal Studios, and Ticketmaster are figuring it out, the smaller companies really struggle with the new technology. It's formidable work and it's more about culture and community than people realize. Most just don't have the insight or resources to weather Web3's volatility the way that we have. I've been interviewed on NPR, by *GQ* magazine, and onstage at conferences like NFT LA and Korea Blockchain Week on our unique journey into crypto. I've headlined Gary Vee's confer-

* By the fall of 2022, the SEC and the U.S. government claimed jurisdiction over the Ethereum network due to its validator nodes being set up within the States.

ence in a Minneapolis football stadium. We've thrown massive parties for our community with Steve Aoki and Pusha T, and produced a live talk show called *Bomb Talk* where I interview friends and special guests in the space. The best part has been forging a new type of camaraderie with our community, where the relationship doesn't feel so lopsided anymore. NFTs have blessed me with a new harvest of lifelong friendships, where I sincerely feel like we are building the future of The Hundreds (and Web3) together.

Yet there have been days where the Discord hate is so suffocating, I'd be willing to give it all back. When you're in crypto (as an investor, as an artist, as an NFT founder), so much of your mental health is tethered to the line that staggers up and down like a drunk stumbling down the street. You don't need an alarm clock when you anxiously scramble to check floor prices as soon as your eyes open. You don't need sleeping pills when your brain just can't take it anymore.

I lost seventeen pounds in that first month after Adam Bomb Squad released. I was a zombie in the days and a vampire in the evenings, depleted by being on-call 24/7 for the community. I felt a personal duty to hold the floor price up and a responsibility to drill for utility like oil. Most of all, I was laden with punishing guilt. Some people lost money by buying bombs too high on the secondary marketplace. Even if they made money, they were incensed that they didn't make more. When a scammer duped our Discord community into buying fake ABS NFTs, we came out of pocket and made everyone whole again to the tune of $100,000. It still wasn't enough and the blame compounded, striking a nerve with all my childhood trauma and savior issues.

By the end of the year, I was seeing my therapist twice a week (no matter how many times I asked, she refused to accept ETH!) due to stress, depression, and debilitating anxiety. She also helped me feel a bit better when I'd sob about NFTs and she'd nod her head knowingly. It was clear that many of her clients were scooping out water in the same boat. The whole thing felt like being locked into a rocket ship that set course for the next ten years. Sometimes it was fun, hopeful, and exhilarating. Most days I wanted to head back home.

Building an NFT collection is like building a company in reverse. You collect all the money upfront and then you spend the rest of your life proving your worth to your customers. The way it's designed now, it's an unpleasant process, if not a doomed model. Founder energy is finite, yet consumer avarice is infinite. If the collector's expectation is to make money from the NFT, no amount of return will ever be satisfactory—which spirals into FUD.* Furthermore, floor prices spend most of their time descending or flatlining, punctuated with spikes of bull runs. So, if the sole purpose of buying the NFT is investment, the majority of the holder's experience monitoring markets will be consumed by worrying about money and wondering when the line will move up again.

Because the thing is—most NFTs aren't designed as in-

---

* Nobody complains more about floor price than the communities whose NFTs are astronomically high. They have the most to lose and the highest stakes. Many of them also came in postmint, betting big to enter the community.

NFTS ARE A SCAM

vestments at all (and if they are, they're not very sound or safe). In 2021, pre-utility-expectations, PFP-style NFTs were intended as collectibles or even novelties. Today, communities place pressure on NFT founders to deliver a future product. That money they spend isn't proffered as an exchange for art or a fun JPEG anymore. It's retroactively framed as an investment in a company, which is an entirely different relationship and dynamic. The fundamental flaw with this? Suddenly, the creators are expected to perform like tested corporations, when most projects are barely start-ups. The founders are also expected to use the "raised funds" to ideate and execute a bottomless bag of brilliant ideas: video games, private clubs, metaverse wearables, and at the very least, hoodies.

Here's the thing. When people grumble about their NFTs—that they aren't providing enough utility or aren't proving to be lucrative investments—what this attitude is really saying is, "I don't actually believe in NFTs." Because in the physical space, the same appeals aren't being made of physical paintings or baseball cards and sneakers. That expectation of further reward proclaims that the NFT is meaningless and valueless on its own, like the paper a stock certificate is printed on. This sentiment betrays a lack of faith in the total picture. And it's troubling that it undergirds the entire system.

My wife was confused. I had been lamenting to her, for the billionth time, how I was having a hard time carrying the burden of the community's anxieties on my back.

"I don't get it. You've never cared like this before. What changed this time?"

"What do you mean?"

"Like, I've never seen you take on responsibility for your customers' decisions like this."

"Sure I have," I defended. "Of course I care about their well-being."

"No, that's not what I'm saying. You're wrestling with some weird guilt thing. Acting like you deceived them or misled them with these NFTs. Do you feel like that?"

"No," I said firmly. "Not at all."

"Really? Then why do you feel bad for these people? They believed in the brand, they admired what you've built, and they wanted to be a part of this. I just don't understand why you feel blameworthy for their choices. You've sold millions of T-shirts for twenty years. Five-hundred-dollar chairs and one-of-one pieces of art and photography. You've convinced people around the world to spend their money on an idea—The Hundreds. What makes this any different?"

She was making a lot of sense. I was behaving like I didn't believe in what we had built—and what we were building—with The Hundreds and Adam Bomb Squad. Throughout 2021, as we conceptualized, designed, edited, and narrated twenty-five thousand NFTs on the Ethereum blockchain, there wasn't a second where I doubted the legitimacy of our product and its intentions. It was the same care, work, and dedication we had invested in our clothing, our retail stores, and our food. Yet I was fretting like any other FUDder, and my actions were loud and clear that I didn't believe in Adam Bomb Squad. I felt like a fraud.

Of course, the truth was that I *did* believe in the work. I was just . . . scared. See, it wasn't just about me anymore. Once daylight pierced the dawn, I realized that I wasn't alone at sea. I was captaining a ship with thousands of passengers. It was one thing to venture into dark waters alone—not only could I handle the journey, I welcomed the uncertain adventure. But if my family and community were in tow, that would radically alter the circumstances and anxieties. I'd be culpable for their safe passage.*

Turns out, I was looking at it all wrong. For the hundredth time, Web3 was swift to humble me. The biggest lesson I've learned in NFTs is that there's a prodigious canyon between consumers and investors. With The Hundreds, my perception of a fan or constituent is someone who is eager to wear the brand in exchange for status and identity. With Adam Bomb Squad, many—if not most—participants aren't retail customers. They might not even be fans. They are investors who see themselves as fractional owners, if not partners.† Instead of seeing that as a burden or taking it on as pressure, with time I reframed my view of our holders as helpers. Every night

---

* Like most artists, I work by myself or with Ben and a small team. The artist's journey is an independent one, isolated and alone. Soloism is conducive to reckless imaginativeness, however, and a wild creativity—because there's no accountability, less at stake, and not much to lose.

Throughout my career, I've shielded myself from feedback as much as possible, staying clear of comments sections and customer complaints. I'm not just insulating myself from the hate, but also the misleading flattery, the unwarranted requests, the peanut gallery grousing, and the backseat driving. Above all, my art isn't unduly swayed by financial pragmatism or confused by business strategies. It's the purest path. The artist roams freely and uninfluenced, being led by his compass alone.

† In NFT land, this transition from consumer/collector to investor marked the move from art to utility.

I logged on to Discord, there were fewer grumblers skulking around. Instead, the new community was happy to greet me, ask how everything was going, and best of all, how they could help. People organized beach bonfires, volunteered T-shirt design ideas, and rendered digital clothing to be worn in the Metaverse. They minted their own POAPs (Proof of Attendance NFTs that are free to mint and like a concert ticket stub souvenir in your scrapbook) and formed their own social clubs offline. Eight thousand five hundred is a lot of mouths to feed, but if harmonized in unison, 8,500 mouths can sing songs of revolution. One of The Hundreds' slogans is "Strength in Numbers" and yet here I was, missing the point completely. I'd written a national bestseller on building a brand around community. Adam Bomb Squad taught me what can happen when the community builds the brand.

I can't think of a tougher and more complicated sector to start up a business than Web3. But that's largely because our business learnings are entrenched in ancient systems and schools of thought. Web3 is established in decentralization and the distribution of power. Meanwhile, success stories historically honor the egotistical and the selfish. Take, for instance, the classic entrepreneurial track. In the Western world, we champion the individual. It's all about the autonomous eagle, breaking free from the convocation and soaring high. We do this even when we know the story tends to end dolefully. The elderly tycoon sits deserted in his chambers on a snowy Christmas morning. "It's lonely at the top." He's stepped on everyone else to climb his mountain peak. Once he arrives, the accomplishment feels hollow because there is no one to share it with.

When Web3 talks about NFTs and community, it's often from the angle of cultivating growth, brand loyalty, and marketing. The paramount benefit of community, however, is that the founder builds a great company in good company. The trailblazing road was never meant to be walked alone. Creation is a collaborative practice and the truest win is one that is distributed and shared. It's a new narrative that only makes more sense as Web3 grows into itself. In the not-so-distant future, we'll look back and scratch our heads that it could've been any other way.

STEVE AOKI

The day I linked with Steve to do this interview, his *Entrepreneur* magazine cover hit the newsstands. The title? "Why Web3? Is it a Business Game-Changer? Cut Through the Hype with Steve Aoki." Just a few weeks prior, Steve passed Snoop Dogg to become the celebrity NFT collector with the most valuable portfolio of over $5 million in digital collectibles. The world-famous DJ isn't like many of the other pop culture personalities who've dipped in and out of the space, hustling cash grabs or losing interest once it came time to cultivate a brand and community. Steve continues to dole out collections under Aokiverse and tie in meaningful utility for his fans. He's the advocate we all need to make the Web2 to Web3 transition seamless.

BOBBY: As an avid collector, tell us about the parallels between NFTs and trading cards.

STEVE: Take the actual card. The value of the card is literally a penny. The cost to make the card is a penny. The cost for a digital piece of art is nothing except how much time the artist took to create the IP and all that stuff that comes into it. So, the actual cost of these things is nothing, right? It's the market that dictates what the card is.

There are cards that are worth nothing and then there's cards that are worth $1 million. They're made of the exact same thing, but you know the market is like, "This card is important to culture." And important to those particular people that love this part of culture. Those people are willing to spend that much money for it. There are enough people that it sustains the marketplace for decades, especially for cards.

When it comes to NFTs, you have the same model but it's brand-new—it's a whole new world. But it's also digging into not just collectors, like people who love cards (the collector mindset is the same)—but you're diving into the crypto space and people who love things that are not alternative to how we see the regulatory process of life. People are excited about that future and where it's going, and it opens up to a new market of people with that same collector mindset.

I'm a collector across the board—whether it's cards, shoes, toys, art, just things that have value to culture or to my nostalgia. I can go into NFTs for many different reasons. One is definitely the collector mindset, for sure. And then there are other things like I was talking about earlier—the excitement of where we're going and being early into something that I feel that's inevitably a part of the way we transact and communicate, socialize, and identify among people who feel the same way.

B: There's a meme-y joke that once Steve Aoki buys into a project, there's a downturn! You're self-aware enough to laugh at it yourself. But public figures do have a critical impact on the marketplace. Celebrities swapping their avatars for an Ape or bomb could have significant results. I assumed it was because there was speculation that mainstream exposure would fuel the brand's notoriety. But can you talk about the role of influencers and celebrities in the ecosystem?

S: Every industry, anyone of any influence, is going to raise attention, whether it's a shampoo or it's NFTs. If you bring in any influential member in any industry, it's like, "Okay, why are they a part of it?" Clearly, when Pepsi brings on Britney Spears, we all know she got paid a lot of money for that, but the Britney Spears fan is now, like, "Oh, I want a Pepsi." It actually has a direct relation to the brand. That's just the way we are as a species—people inspire us and what they do will engage with how we think about what we want to do.

Potentially, in that space, that does have an unconscious effect on our decisions in every aspect. NFTs for sure, but it's way more—it's a smaller specific pool of people who are investing in the Web3 NFT space. You can't just throw any celebrity into this space and it will work. It has to be in this high mind of those people that feel like it does have a real influence in their culture. So, it's like you have someone that's clearly a celebrity in the world, but you realize they don't really have an impact on this small little world. It might have an opposite reaction of an impact that might attract away from the project. Sometimes, the smallest names doing incredible things have the largest impact. Certain celebrities can definitely move the needle for sure, one hundred percent. But I say the majority of them can't. Because they're not hitting the mark with the people that are investing. It's a much more educated crowd than, say, a Coca-Cola brand partnership, where it's a passive crowd with billions of people.

B: Like me, you walked into this space with a sizable audience that is not only unfamiliar with crypto culture but perhaps even opposed to it. How have you navigated this conversation? Do you feel like you have to code-switch between audiences? Or are you insistent that since you live comfortably in both worlds, your fans should also?

S: There's going to be a disconnect. It's like what I was talking about with this Pepsi world and this NFT world—it's a small community, I'm not going to target everyone. I'm not going to speak to everyone about NFTs. I am going to let the world know, "Hey, I'm involved in Web3, I'm involved in NFTs"—I really am. I'm a believer in the space, but I'm not going to go into high-level conversation. You have to know who you're speaking to and know how to speak the language and gauge the interest level. The better you understand that, then the better you can have more meaningful conversation and discourse.

Especially on a subject like Web3—onboarding that space is already a bit higher level than onboarding into a new cultural movement of music or something. Or, for you, with clothing—you have different ways of speaking the brand of The Hundreds. There's a high-level brand, of having conversation for the deep streetwear heads, and there are people that just want The Hundreds T-shirts.

Your influence in Web3 has always been inspirational to me. When I saw you enter the space, it was really informative, insightful, educational, and definitely inspiring how you integrated The Hundreds and what you're doing with that community and having a successful launch with the Adam Bomb Squad. I just thought what you did was really well done and inclusive, fun, and engaging. It's really great.

B: Thanks, man. Okay, so one of the recurring topics in Web3 is music NFTs, and there have been various takes on it. It's a broader question, but how do you feel about this pressure to solve a lot of the music industry's issues with NFTs? Personally speaking, I haven't seen enough convincing answers or offerings to date, but have you?

S: I feel like we're at that stage where . . . You know that movie *Who Killed the Electric Car?* There's a guy that's like, "Yo, you can make cars electric, how cool is that?" and he just came in and said, "Fuck that, I'm buying shit" and just burned it, and it's a whole fucking story. They're like, "There's no way there's an electric car, the car industry will never allow that to happen." And, inevitably, the major automobile industry started making electric cars because you have a guy like Elon Musk that created Tesla. And then GM and Ford were like, "Fuck it, we're in." You know?

We're at that stage right now with music NFTs. It's too soon to put music on the blockchain right now—it will disrupt so much of how things work from a major-label perspective and how the world works with the artists' and labels' relationship and royalty structure and how all that works. We're still at that stage. There's too many blockages and blockades to get there. But we will get there. I think it's inevitable that music will live on the blockchain and that we'll have this more transparent smart contract of money distribution, because that obviously benefits artists. It's going to happen. There's just powers that be that are too strong right now, and eventually there will be some sort of innovation.

I think the thing with Web3 and NFTs and what we're doing in the traditional world with fashion and music—and how we buy and sell and live in that world—it's still very clunky. The onboarding, once that gets smoothed out—it's as easy to put money in the bank or get money out or do things like that where it's not dangerous. People are terrified. They're scared. When it becomes more normal how to buy things or trade things or live in that space in Web3—that's the first step. Second, it's having a visionary, like the people who created Spotify. Like people who created iTunes on Apple when it was all physical. There's going to be something like that. That'll happen and then it'll be very normal to see music NFTs. At one point, you go back in time, people were like, "Why would I buy a digital download for ninety-nine cents?! I need to hold the CD.

This is crazy and for a digital download—you spend ninety-nine cents for a digital download that goes into an iPod? That's so absurd. Let alone stream it." With any new technology of how we listen or buy things or wear things or whatever it is—it's always this absurdity of what the future is to a majority of people. And then there's this small percentage of people who are like, "Well, we think this is how it's going to be."

B: Are you as bullish on NFTs at the end of 2022 as you were in early 2021? Why or why not?

S: Haha, that's a funny one! Alright, so 2021 . . . it just won't happen again, you know? That run, it's like this analogy—"Shit, there's gold in California!" and everyone's rushing. It's like the Wild Wild West, Oregon Trail, and then hey, it's tapped out! What are we going to do? Now we're stuck here and there's no more gold, no more rush. It's over. But guess what? California was born!

B: That's such great way to put it!

S: With the rush, you have a lot of people, right? And a lot of people, they just care about making money because they see it. It's like the big new headline: "How do we make money fast and get the fuck out?" There are a lot of people like that. It fucks up the whole ecosystem when you have too many of those people, now since the market is so down, you can't do that anymore. There's no room for that. So the only people that are actually in the space are people that actually care.

We are living in California now. We've already put our forts up. We're already building here. We're the people that have real longevity and real interest to see it go for a long time. Those are the ones that have a real stake in the economy and to grow that space. A lot of them will die out, and it's going to be exactly how it is and how the markets work when you open a restaurant. Nine out of ten of them fail. When you open a nightclub, nine out of ten of them fail. When you open a new business in the real world, it's very difficult. You have to bring a real service to your community or else it won't work. And that's just how we are entering into the space of Web3, with NFTs, whatever it is that we build in that space. It's not going to be easy to build and make money. You have to do it for real. It makes you have to fucking care to spend the time to put in there, to put your time investment and financial investment in, because you believe in it and you actually want to grow it. Some of those businesses will work. Just like in the real world, someone will come up to me like, "Hey, should I open up a restaurant in Las Vegas?" I'm like, I don't know, I'm just going to tell you the statistics—nine out of ten are going to fail, now go ahead. So, if you really want to know that and if you really fucking love cooking or making food then do it, but it's not easy. You know what I mean?

B: Speaking of which, you were one of the first celebrities I remember minting NFTs, and you continue to pour yourself into the A0K1VERSE. Most don't realize how hard it is to run these projects. Your manager, Matt, saw me the morning after Adam Bomb Squad released and said, "The real work begins now." Tell us what it's like as an NFT project founder and

NFTS ARE A SCAM

how you've managed to sustain and thrive in this industry.

S: Oh my god, AOK1VERSE is a full-time operation, we have a full-time staff and team and even with everything that's going on with FTX and with crypto down, we are full steam ahead. The staff is working on all cylinders. Aokiverse is a tier system; we have different levels. The highest level, level six, is people that bought over one thousand Aoki credits. A credit is about 0.1 ETH or whatever that value is. When it was moving before, it was a healthy amount of money, and one thing with level six is that I have to do a song with the numbers, and I never open that kind of doorway to anyone. But I really care about the AOK1VERSE Web3 community. And I want to bring something to the table. Just a few days ago, I made a banger with one of the numbers.

B: Really? Tell me about that.

S: Played it live at my show, together! So I'm fulfilling all those things that I'm doing. We're making NFTs with numbers and I spend a lot of time just to get to the stage where I can actually make those NFTs. It's taken six to eight months to get there because they're going to be amazing. They're just really incredible NFTs. On my creative side, me personally, I put in a tremendous amount of work. On the team side, you already know how much time we put into the community, and our staff. In many ways, I'm not making money on any of it. We put so much money back into everything to be fulfilled. It's time and money. I don't need to do it. I truly don't need to do it. I'm successful, doing what I do. Do I need to do it for money? No, I actually don't.

B: Same, same.

S: You do it because you care about where we're going. We're excited about innovating, about our communities doing something new. And that's why you're Bobby Hundreds and that's why I'm Steve Aoki—because we put ourselves on the line to build things from the ground up and create communities. And if we make money in the end, that's great. But we make a healthy community out of what we do. That's the most fulfilling, satisfying part of why I do what I do, and I'm sure it's the same thing for you.

B: Love it. Final question! Are NFTs a scam?

S: YES!

B: That's the best answer I've gotten so far!

S: Oh god, that's a good one! I'm going to be the cover of your book! I better be on the cover of your booking saying, "Yes, they're a scam!"

B: Steve, are NFTs a scam?

S: No, of course anything in art, in collectibles, there's always a bad actor—that's a very common word you hear in Web3. There's always the dangers, but in everything we do moving forward in the evolution of life and technological progress of how we communicate and socialize with and identify with things, there's always going to be people doing some evil shit, and they're going to benefit off others and just bounce. It's happened with every single technological progression. We've seen it before, many times—it's never going to be one hundred percent just like harmony and butterflies and all that good stuff and unicorns.

There are good people doing good shit and there's bad people doing bad shit. But with everything, there's always intention. I think very positively about the human race and I'm very optimistic. My general sense of humans is that they're going to be more good than bad. You just need to identify and differentiate and learn and educate yourself on what you put your time into. And who you're going to align yourself with, you know? That's life. This is not just an NFT question; this is a life question. Everything is a scam at some level, in some industry—there's always a scam element in everything that we pour ourselves into. And there's always the reason why we do it. Follow that and align yourself with like-minded people.

NFTS ARE FOREVER

On November 7, 2022, The Hundreds dropped its second NFT collection, entitled Badam Bomb Squad, amid a dreary bear market, the FTX scandal, and in the face of a global recession. With overall NFT sales volume hitting consistent all-time lows, some questioned why we were creating a second installment of bombs. At the time, it wasn't customary for artists and founders to keep producing NFTs unless their existing collections were commanding exorbitant resale prices. I couldn't help but think how this type of crypto myopia was limiting the space and hanging a short ceiling over the NFT market. In my opinion, the only thing that could save NFTs was more NFTs.

After our first NFT collection, Adam Bomb Squad, debuted in the summer of 2021, I was faced with myriad responses from spectators. There were those who were quick to congratulate us, others who were eager to hate. More than anything, I was met with a lot of questions. "I don't really get the whole crypto thing, but seems like you guys pulled off something cool?" Of all the comments, however, none was more amusing than friends and customers asking, "They sold out too fast! Can you give me a heads-up on the next release?"

With The Hundreds, we'd conditioned our community to anticipate scheduled drops. Every season, we offer a new collection of clothing in stores. Every other week, we market another fun collaboration or special project. Once twenty-five thousand Adam Bomb Squad NFTs sold out in forty minutes, the sophisticated NFTers knew to flock to auction sites like OpenSea to buy a bomb from a reseller. But our non-NFT crowd wanted to purchase the collectible directly from us, the source, whether due to authentication, for the emotional experience, or to be the original owner. ("I'll just wait for the next one!")

I had to explain to our community that when it comes to NFTs, the point is to keep reselling and buying into the *same* collection. Reason being that the Web3 collectibles system is engineered so that most projects continue to promote—and profit off—their existing NFTs instead of consistently dropping new ones. NFT creators (of the "PFP" variety à la sports cards) generate money in two ways. First, they "mint out" of a collection, meaning they make a certain number of NFTs, price them accordingly, and sell them out online. Pretty straightforward.

The second way that artists and founders make money off their NFTs is by getting a cut of every resale forever. NFTs are designed to be scarce and sell out immediately and that drives energy toward the secondary market. This part is reminiscent of trading models you often see with streetwear, Pokémon cards, and blue-chip art, except in those cases, the creator doesn't typically benefit from secondary sales of their pieces. In Web3, however, one of the paradigm's fundamental promises is that every time an artist's NFT changes hands in the marketplace, they still get a cut of that resale thanks to smart contracts. The objective is to keep the demand up around an NFT collection as traders shuffle around the same collectibles and the original creator is rewarded a percentage of every flip.

Although this model has proven to be effective with some prominent NFT collections, it can be limiting, not only for the brands but for the overall space. Imagine there being only one neighborhood in the world. In the beginning, fifty houses for fifty families would suffice. Over time, the demand for that short supply of homes would rise with population growth. There would come a point when those fifty houses would be out of reach for 99.9 percent of people. This might mean some jaw-dropping sales figures for those homes, but it would not do much for the "mass adoption" of houses. Those fortunate fifty residents would carry on the game among themselves, but the other 99.9 percent would lose interest and seek another venue that could accommodate them.

The mistake that many have made in NFTs is misunderstanding the scarcity model. Oftentimes, founders and NFT creators aspire to be like luxury brands that limit the supply of a product to heighten its allure. They believe that to build a sought-after NFT brand, the number of NFTs should be restricted (and they justify this decision by the high prices some of those NFTs currently achieve at auction). Yet there may be good reason for making more NFTs to build a bigger brand and a more expansive ecosystem. The New York skate brand Supreme didn't just make one collection of clothing in the nineties and cash in their chips. While the specific pieces within seasonal drops are limited, *the drops themselves are limitless.* Supreme, as a brand, is perpetually printing shirts, stocking their online shop, hyping hot collaborations, and replenishing their customers' closets. Supreme is infinite. They have become one of the most mainstream and notorious fashion brands in the world. And yet, they still maintain an exclusive aura and command an impressive resale value around individual clothing items.

With traditional collectibles, the goal is not only to keep the demand around the product up, but to reinforce the brands dealing the limited goods, and above all, to support the space itself. This is accomplished by converting more collectors, regularly issuing collectibles, and segmenting product for different markets. Pokémon didn't stop with their first trading card game set in 1996. Today, they have nearly one hundred editions in circulation with varying price points. And most artists don't dedicate their entire career to promoting the same series of paintings to their buyers. They'd rather be prolific, constantly producing and adding texture to their legacy.

In 1985, Nike released the very first Air Jordan to the public for $65. They anticipated selling 100,000 pairs by year's end but wound up selling 450,000 in the first month alone. The shoe was so surprisingly popular that Nike overshot production on the Jordan I and flooded the market. Prices plummeted. Sales racks were soon filled with Nike Air Jordans. (In fact, the "I" was adopted as the first skate shoe in the eighties—not just for its agile design and ankle protection, but because the footwear was so affordable for skaters.) Still, Nike followed up the Air Jordan I with the Air Jordan II the next November. Almost every year since, Nike's released another new Jordan design, even long after its namesake, Michael Jordan, retired from basketball. The Air Jordan XXXVII was recently unveiled and can be purchased on Nike's website for $185, with some sizes of the popular colorways already sold out.

Nike wouldn't have had the same meteoric rise in the eighties and ensuing decades if it weren't for the Air Jordan. And sneaker collecting wouldn't have become a $72 billion industry if it weren't for Nike. Nike alone makes up $34 billion of that number and, at fifty-eight years old, is regarded as one of the most valuable brands in the world. Imagine an alternate universe where Nike stopped shoe production after the first Jordan hit the clearance corner. Eventually, those Jordan I's might have fetched a high resale value for a niche group of collectors trading among themselves. Over time, however, without the infrastructure of a global brand like Nike, an endless stream of fresh designs, a culture, and a broader audience, the mystique and enthusiasm around those sneakers would have crumbled like a decomposing midsole.

There's another, more urgent reason why we need more NFTs to save NFTs.

We're at a crossroads with NFTs whereby the default royalties model for secondary sales is being questioned, if not abolished. To stay competitive in a crypto slump, marketplaces like X2Y2, Magic Eden, and LooksRare have all recently chosen to abandon the required standard. Instead of marketplaces enforcing royalties for artists, they are leaving it to the collectors to decide if they'd prefer to pay the creators. While this about-face is antithetical to Web3's ethos, many are surrendering to the sobering truth that this is the inevitable trajectory for NFTs. The royalties cut for creators and founders was always a charitable bonus versus a pinned stipulation.

If OpenSea, the biggest marketplace for NFTs, also pivots to zero-royalties, there could be dire ramifications for digital collectibles. One worry is that project founders will desert their projects. Without any future revenue coming in from royalties, there is little incentive to continue pumping secondary sales of those NFTs. Not to mention once founders burn through all the original mint money, they won't be able to sustain the business. If founders stop replenishing perks and utility for their holders, enthusiasm or hopefulness for those projects may wither.

In the late 1990s, professional musicians were faced with extinction once MP3s and Napster were invented, but they adjusted by making money off their art in other ways beyond CD and cassette sales. They leaned on touring, merch, and licensing deals. Today, the music industry is still very much alive and thriving, even though it looks different from generations past. Artists and founders in NFTs will also be pushed to adapt and rewrite the rules, just like they've done many times before. Perhaps project communities will find ways to aggregate their own funds to keep the energy up around the brand. Maybe NFT creators will restrict trading of their NFTs to their own personalized marketplaces, ensuring that they receive cuts of the secondary market.

There are solutions for NFT creators trying to survive in the face of zero-royalties marketplaces. While royalties may die, mints are here to stay. Historically, founders are expected to produce collections sparingly, far and few between. Maybe this is because of the CryptoPunks paradigm that most PFP-style NFTs are modeled after. Larva Labs released the Punks in 2017 and never followed it up with a sequel. (I'm not including Meebits.) Instead of looking at mints as a one-and-done, however, what if a brand's drops could be continuous and often, just like sneakers or cards or seasonal streetwear ranges or traditional art (or practically most consumer goods)? This could even finally answer the unrelenting "Wen Utility?" question begged of NFT brands.* Instead of pressuring founders to find limitless ways for their NFTs to dance, perhaps their purpose is in the central thesis: making NFTs. Keep in mind that the biggest collectibles companies (Topps, Great American Coin Company, Funko) serve to print collect-

---

* Many collectors treat NFTs as investments, expecting the resale value of their NFTs to increase according to the artist's or company's growth. The frustration is, however, that most collectors have no idea what they're investing in and for legal reasons, most founders can't share their objectives. There are NDAs to consider, strategic marketing rollouts, and in America, any promise of utility or road map rubs up against a securities risk (the NFT is behaving like a stock).

Even when utility is handed over, it's never enough, because the money that comes with it is never enough. The demand for utility is not necessarily about the utility itself, but the market pump that the hope of utility foments. This devolves into a maddening game for all parties, by which founders are feverishly working on future projects that their community may not actually want. Meanwhile, the NFT holders' insatiable appetite for higher returns is boundless and directionless.

Meanwhile, the rebuttal you often see from the purist NFT community is, "Art doesn't need utility," or in the immortal words of the photographer Drift, "Utility this, utility that. Utility deez nuts fr." It's a fair point. Traditional art, in and of itself, is the reward—its decorativeness, beauty, and thought-provoking nature. Meanwhile, its value is a separate thing, informed by the past and built off the back of the artist's legacy (while NFTs' value is driven by what's projected for the future).

ibles. It's counterintuitive, but their cards, coins, and toys become more special and in-demand the more they make.

All NFTs have intrinsic utility: to be collectible! What makes them valuable, however, has more to do with the theater, history, and reputation of the brand backing the collectible than any of its features or add-ons. For Soho House patrons, the membership card is *useful* because it grants access to an elevator upstairs. The card is *valuable* because of the prestige encircling the Soho House name. Oil brushed across canvas isn't remarkable, but when it's associated with the repertoire and life story of a Van Gogh, the painting becomes precious. And the more Marvel characters are added to the MCU, the more complex Iron Man becomes, and the more significant his franchise.

Consider a preface to a book without a body or epilogue. You need to write more chapters not only to tell a complete story but to make the preface make sense. The suggestion of adding more layers to an NFT brand isn't just to weave a stronger brand narrative, though. It's to also boost the value of the existing collections. Take Rolex, for example. Since they first introduced the popular Daytona in 1963, they've gone from collecting dust in shop windows to being one of the most sought-after retro watches in the world. Over the generations, as newer editions have hit the market with state-of-the-art mechanics and updated designs, the older, hand-wound Paul Newman 6239s with smaller 37mm cases have become romanticized. And scroll back to the bargain-bin Air Jordans. The culture needed Jordan Xs, XXs, and XXXs so that Jordan I's, with their yellowing and cracked leather, could become idealized and sacred. The shoe's scarcity and story are fundamental to its desirability, but its early position on the sneaker timeline has made it one of the most iconic collectibles of all time. In 1985, the first Air Jordan was discounted for $25. Today, the average price for a pair is $25,000.

The critical ingredient across most every valuable collectible is nostalgia. Baseball cards were originally sturdy slabs of cardboard inserted into cigarette boxes to keep the cigarettes from breaking. It took decades for the sport to grow and baseball enthusiasts to develop fandom with their favorite players so that hoarding picture cards became a sentimental hobby. The retro Nike market obviously didn't exist in the early 1980s. The Dunks and Air Maxes we have fond feelings for forty years later were cutting-edge designs at the time. Throughout our lives, the consistent reissues and remodels of those shoes have intersected with different emotional touchpoints, making the shoe much more than leather and laces bound to our feet.

With regard to NFTs, the hard pill to swallow here is that nostalgia takes time and work, while many are here for a hot trade and to conveniently get rich quick. NFTs are still so close to our noses, that they're not even fully defined. You see the Twitter Spaces and think pieces— we're still in the exploratory and educational phase of a new technology. Unfortunately, that also means we don't have enough distance from NFTs to indulge in longing or memory. That also means that if we want this to become anything of meaningful and sustainable value, we have to let it grow authentically, support and participate in the culture, and most of all, believe in it.

In other words, we've gotta be invested.

NFTS AREN'T DEAD

The most exciting part about NFTs is also the most harrowing. Everything just moves so damn fast. Days after I finished writing "NFTs Are Forever," the apparition I was most worried about started materializing: the end of creator royalties. If I were to keep adding chapters for every monumental affair in crypto, this book would never get finished. But I thought this would be the perfect note to end on, to show how NFTs are simultaneously fragile and resilient. The more that NFTs are tested and emerge victorious, the more they are sheathed in a husk of scar tissue. The more breakthroughs are braided into their history, the clearer and more solidified their future becomes . . .

It was only fitting that NFTs would die on a trip to Disneyland—while I was with a group of NFT artists and personalities at that. We'd gathered at an Anaheim theme park because some of our international friends were in town. In fact, I was standing behind Betty from Deadfellaz in line for the Incredicoaster when I got the email. OpenSea, the biggest NFT marketplace, had something very urgent to talk about. No, my assistant texted me, it could not wait.

"Weird, OpenSea needs to talk to me."

"Right now?" Betty asked. "Why'd they wait until Friday afternoon?"

I left my camera off on the Zoom, partially because I was embarrassed that I was taking a meeting while eating a frozen chocolate banana in front of a Spider-Man show. I was also anxious. On Monday, we were partnered with OpenSea to launch our second, highly anticipated collection, titled Badam Bomb Squad. For months, we'd been working closely with OpenSea to debut a new set of five thousand NFTs. Although OpenSea has built a name around being the most popular home for secondary NFT sales, they had recently started a program where they'd work with select artists and founders to push primary drops. The marketing exposure was priceless, and we were honored to be one of the first to be handpicked for the campaign.

Our OpenSea meetings were typically fun and light. Both parties were excited to announce the partnership (especially because we were introducing "collector royalties," an experimental mechanism whereby holders of our original Adam Bomb Squad NFTs would receive royalties alongside us as their Badam Bomb Squad NFTs traded in the market). This time, however, the OpenSea team looked dour on the other side of the screen. They broke the ice by saying they'd figured out a solution to a worrying issue that had been bubbling up with NFTs over the past several months. As crypto and NFTs slumped into a bear market, OpenSea's competitors had made a sharp turn on the standard royalties model in which creators receive a cut every time their work trades between collectors. Most creators relied on these ongoing payments to survive, but LooksRare, X2Y2, Blur, and Magic Eden were trying to win the marketplace wars by reducing royalties, leaving them up to the buyers to pay, or dumping them altogether. NFTs were now cheaper to buy on their platforms, and buyers were quickly figuring it out.

Aside from cheating creators out of their dues, the abolition of royalties beckoned a broader existential threat to Web3. Creator royalties are fundamental to the NFT ethos. Most artists and founders were drawn to Web3 because they didn't benefit off secondary sales of their work in traditional industries. With the advent of smart contracts, artists wouldn't get screwed out of royalties. But if OpenSea embraced this new race-to-the-bottom trend, that would unravel much of the NFT ideology.

As I was on the Zoom with OpenSea, I watched the rollercoaster twist and turn above my head, the squealing of grinding metal infused with the laughter and screams of the passengers. My guts felt like a gnarled amusement park ride as well. Something about this call felt ominously wrong. The OpenSea guys buried the lede, gleefully reporting to us that they'd devised a smart contract tool for all future NFT collections that would enforce trading exclusively on marketplaces that honored creator royalties. Ben and I were texting each other on the side: "Something seems off..."

"Good to hear, but what about past collections? Like Adam Bomb Squad?" we asked.

"Right now, we don't have a solution for NFTs that

already exist, unless they have an upgradable contract in which we can embed this code."

But we didn't have that for Adam Bomb Squad. In fact, nobody we knew with an existing NFT collection had an upgradable contract. In the spirit of immutability, most projects would have been crucified for an open contract until that point. It slowly dawned on us that OpenSea was considering dropping creator royalties for existing collections. They were set to publish their official announcement on Monday, giving space for everyone to voice their opinions before making a final decision in one month. This was bad news, not just for our partnership (we'd be crossing the picket line if we sided with OpenSea over the artists) and for Adam Bomb Squad (which survives off royalties), but for the future of all NFTs.

"Bobby, what's going on?" Betty inquired. She could read the bewildered look on my face as I imagined the erosive ripples from OpenSea's pending announcement. We were climbing into the Incredicoaster cars, but I couldn't enjoy the moment.

"I have a feeling that OpenSea's gonna follow the other marketplaces and ditch creator royalties also," I muttered, just quietly enough so our other NFT friends couldn't hear. Technically, and legally, I was still under an NDA and was only privy to this information because of our OpenSea relationship. They'd asked that we keep this information close to our chest until their statement on Monday, but in our defense, they had broken our trust first. Earlier in the week, Ben had signed our finalized contracts with OpenSea when they were already contemplating this decision, leaving us effectively in the dark. Plus, leading up to this, we had asked them whether there was any consideration of moving to zero royalties, and they'd told us it wasn't on the boards.

After we got off the ride, I headed directly for the park exits. Disneyland had lost its sparkle, and nothing is more annoying than being trapped inside the Happiest Place on Earth when your world is crashing down. That evening, Ben and I pulled a few of our smartest NFT friends, like ThankYouX, Farokh, Richerd from Manifold, Betty, Matt Colon, Naveen of Yat, and FVCKRENDER, into a group chat to devise a game plan. How do we get in front of this? Is there a solution? At first, it was a moment for fellow founders and artists to air their grievances. For years, OpenSea, as a platform, had been reticent and disconnected from the creator community. They asked artists to consult for them without pay. They were slow to fix things and hard to communicate with. Meanwhile, they'd raised $300 million at a $13 billion valuation in January 2022. OpenSea was a convenient and bloated target. Did they really need to cut royalties to survive against their competitors? Hadn't they made enough money by taking a cut of our sales for so long? When I spoke with Gordon Goner about this, he stated that OpenSea had never once bothered to reach out to the Bored Apes founders. Meanwhile, their umbrella corporation, Yuga Labs, is responsible for most of the trading volume on the website.

I did my best to compartmentalize my negative feelings about OpenSea and not conflate one complaint for another. For one, I was frustrated that our drop was now compromised. We'd worked hard on Badam Bomb Squad and had built the release into an already busy schedule.

Now we were thinking of moving the drop to another marketplace so that we weren't endorsing OpenSea's actions, but that would require all new web design and smart contracts. I was worried about the health of Adam Bomb Squad if royalties were shut off. We had made a sizable sum off of our primary mint, but that budget could only take us so far. Consistent royalties justified working on the collection, from marketing to events to added utility. Without them, it would be impossible to continue the project. Above all, I was upset that OpenSea was jeopardizing this social contract that most of us had upon adopting NFTs—fairness and equity for artists. The arrangement around creator royalties was even stipulated in clear terms on OpenSea's own website. It seemed unfair and unethical to pull the rug out on this promise.

Word soon leaked around the creator community, and OpenSea was forced to rush out the announcement via Twitter on Saturday night. I'm not sure if they were intentionally trying to muddy the conversation, but judging from the replies, most people who read OpenSea's tweet thread were confused. The unclear language left the impression that OpenSea had invented a tool that would not only protect creator royalties for future projects but also existing collections as well. This wasn't true, and so I did my best to clarify OpenSea's stance in an elaborate series of tweets. Gordon Goner wrote a blog post suggesting a solution in which a council of NFT leaders (like a DAO) would greenlight which marketplaces we should all sell on as a united front. The artist FEWOCiOUS handwrote a testimony of how invaluable creator royalties are to the movement. Betty mobilized hundreds of artists and founders

NFTS ARE A SCAM

in her DMs. We also started speaking up on live Twitter Spaces roundtables in front of audiences to get the word out. Sometimes the heads of OpenSea would even join to hear the community or defend their choices. On Tuesday, Farokh hosted a Rug Radio Spaces in which he invited me, Betty, and ThankYouX to face the cofounder and CEO of OpenSea, Devin Finzer, in front of thousands of people.

After a spirited, but heated, dialogue, I told the OpenSea team, "Look, none of us are saying you started the fire. But you're the ones holding the fire hose." And then I went on to half-jokingly quote Uncle Ben from Spider-Man: "With great power comes great responsibility."

When I really sat and thought about it, however, OpenSea didn't have great power at all. OpenSea had great money, great brand awareness, and were leaders in the NFT marketplace wars. But their power was actually derived from the artists, founders, and brands whose work was trading on their forums. Without us, our contributions, and our support, they had very little power. The only reason why they had the upper hand to make decisions over us is because we—the creators—were fragmented. A couple seasons back, we printed a Hundreds T-shirt that was inspired by a quote from the cult L.A. gangster film *Blood In Blood Out*. It read, ONCE WE GET TOGETHER, THEY DON'T RUN SHIT. It reminded me that if artists and founders band together and speak up in unison, we can move mountains.

That night, I published a press release across our social media channels. In solidarity with our fellow creators, we were severing our partnership with OpenSea and launching our new collection ourselves through our own website. Although we had just locked ourselves into a deal with the marketplace to conduct all our primary drops for the next year, we wanted to take a stand for independence and the independents. Web3's ethos is anchored in decentralization, sovereignty, and ownership. The entire point is not having to rely on an institution or corporation. Although the marketing exposure of big gatekeepers helps, NFTs are a disruptive and revolutionary technology by which the creators can sell directly to their supporters without the need of an intermediary. All you need is to code a widget into your web page. We trusted that our community of collectors would find us if we dropped Badam Bomb Squad via our own venue. It was a symbolic gesture. I signed the note with the declaration, "The artists are always in control."

The following afternoon, at two, OpenSea scheduled a wrap-up call with us. We didn't quite know what the meeting was about outside of closing our contract. Their countenances were much more animated as the Zoom opened on their conference room. After we exchanged pleasant catch-ups, one of the OpenSea representatives cleared the air.

"I've just gotta say this," one chuckled to himself. He then exhaled, "Where the hell were you all the last few months while everyone else was cutting their royalties!?"

We all laughed. It was a valid point. Web3's dark secret is that creator royalties are a social construct—a gift from the marketplaces—versus firm truth. With NFTs, it's not unusual for collectors to swap collectibles outside of marketplaces, through agents like NFT Trader or directly with one another, to avoid fees. In the past, most creators didn't take it too seriously, however, as that type of buying and selling wasn't happening at scale. And as the smaller marketplaces quietly adopted this crooked model, many of us didn't treat it like a significant threat, even if it registered on everyone's anxiety radar. OpenSea, with its size and presence, however, could tip the balance and end royalties once and for all.

"We just wanted to be the ones to tell you that Open-Sea will continue to honor royalties for all NFTs, both future and present," they said.

I wish someone had been recording this Zoom or that I was quick enough to screen-grab our responses. But I couldn't, because my jaw was on the table and my body was immobilized. Ben, Sandy, and I were speechless, the faint hum of room tone filling in the blanks. If you didn't know any better, it looked like our connection had frozen.

"I'm sorry," I tripped, "I'm confused. Can you repeat that?"

"Yeah, nothing's changing. We're keeping royalties, even for existing collections. In fact, as we're telling you this, we're tweeting it live."

I toggled my screen to a browser and pulled up my Twitter stream. Sure enough, just seconds prior, OpenSea had dropped a scroll explaining their intent to preserve creator royalties and advocate for artists and founders. My texts, WhatsApp, and Telegram were erupting.

"Wow. Umm . . . thank you?"

OpenSea asked us to reconsider dropping our collection with them and then the meeting ended. Just like that.

"Now. What. The. Hell. Was. That. All. About?!" I cried out in exasperation. We'd just wasted so much time, and now, out of principle, we were without a home for our NFT project. We were set to drop our collection the very next day but had stalled on all marketing fronts and weren't prepared for the release. What's worse, I felt like we had done all this free consulting work for OpenSea by being the pawn in their decision-making process. To us, it felt like they had used us to test out the public reaction and gracefully walked their statements back once they saw the backlash. We were depleted.

It was the most bizarre feeling. Like being thrown in at the last minute for a championship boxing fight on the world's stage, only to train your hardest, get into the ring, and realize that your opponent had forfeited. Once again, OpenSea had got us all worked up and overwrought for nothing. I closed my office blinds, locked my door, and slouched in my chair for the next two hours, sapped of energy. I could barely muster replying to the congratulatory DMs and heart-ing gracious tweets.

The next morning, Ben got on a call with the OpenSea team and politely declined the offer to return to their platform. And over the next week—no exaggeration—almost every marketplace reached out to host our drop for free, many of which had never bothered to connect with us before. Some offered money; some dangled other carrots to sweeten the deal. We had the juice, and they were now trying to use us as pawns in their own agenda. Ben and I stuck to our guns, however, and ultimately minted Badam Bomb Squad on our site two weeks later. The collection didn't sell out at the rate we had hoped it would, and perhaps it really would have moved faster if a marketplace had promoted it. But it was a win for Web3. Plus, our core community showed up for us. The ones we wanted in. And the right ones acknowledged what we had done. We figured that value would circle back around to us in another shape or form one day.

All this creator-royalties drama was going down against the backdrop of a much more chaotic and alarming story unfurling that same day: the collapse of FTX, the eventual airing-out of its fraudulent founder, Sam Bankman-Fried, and the undoing of crypto. It also happened to be America's midterm elections on Tuesday. There was a blood moon overhead, daylight saving time was disturbing our sleep, and at home, my son was deep in basketball try-outs for his middle school team, probably the most topical event of all.

Most days I'm driving home from the office, I look at the drivers to the left and right of me on the freeway and think about how they'll never know any of this happened. Then I wonder what is consuming them. What have they been working on today, what are they daydreaming about, what are they trying to solve? On tough days, I envy that they'll never know what it's like to be FUDded by disgruntled collectors on Discord or have an occlusion error on 3D rendered generative art. On hopeful days, I allow myself to fantasize that we'll be recognized for our contributions, but of course not. LOL. We're so early. History will bury this prequel to a fantastic story that we've only barely teased a trailer of. I also think about the nameless individuals who poured themselves into the early internet, foundational crypto, and even guys like Matt and John of Larva Labs/CryptoPunks who go uncelebrated while later generations reap the benefits of their risk-taking and hard-fought battles. Maybe this time it'll be different. This time, it's supposed to be different.

Even though no one here will get the credit, that's how much it means to us. That's how much of it is driven by unbridled passion and a belief in something greater.

A couple weeks later, the marketplace X2Y2 broadcasted that—in light of OpenSea's decision—they too would be making the conscious decision to preserve creator royalties for all collections. This was another massive plot twist, considering X2Y2 was partly the reason why zero royalties even entered the chat. It seemed that creator royalties would live to see another day. Either way, I'd played my part. I had a role in that story line and fulfilled it, and the entire space lurched forward another yard for it. Thousands, millions of others do the same in Web3 every single day. Sometimes they get pushed to the front lines, sometimes they're pushing from the back. But the creators, the collectors, the marketplaces, the media, the influencers, the scammers, the FUDders, and the flippers. We're out here, putting in the work.

After I took that OpenSea Zoom meeting at Disneyland, I was immediately strapped and buckled into my roller-coaster seat. The Incredicoaster at California Adventure is a bit of an anomalous experience for the theme park, as it's a full-scale, Six Flags–style ride with a loop, steep drops, and corkscrew turns. As a teenager, I was obsessed with rollercoasters and was even escorted out of Magic Mountain for undoing my safety restraints and free falling on Colossus. Rollercoasters are fun for young people because they can throw their entire bodies into them, their pasts and futures, with abandon. As I've gotten older, however, the experience has gotten more nerve-racking as I've become more fearful, anxious, and have something to lose. After the Incredicoaster does one spin, it returns to home base, where the conductor asks if everyone wants to go again. Whether you like it or not, the answer is always yes. The second time around is even more exhilarating (or painful) because you can't leave.

Crypto and NFTs are a rollercoaster.

There are some days when I just want the rollercoaster to end. Then there are days when I remind myself that this is the exciting part. I recently returned to Disneyland, this time with my kids. My younger son was apprehensive about boarding Space Mountain. He was deathly afraid of the speed, the darkness. Not being able to see where he was going was terrifying. I explained that we're used to understanding fear and fun as two separate things, when they're very much symbiotic. Haunted houses are fun because they're scary, but so are action sports and going on a blind date. And so is gambling. Initially, I wanted to title this book "The Biggest Bet," because I was fascinated— dumbstruck—by how hard people were wagering on NFTs. It wasn't just about investing in PFPs with ETH. People were pivoting careers, swapping friends out, and committing their identities to NFTs. Gary Vee reiterated that he had put his legacy on the line. The world's biggest corporations like Nike, Disney, Starbucks, and Meta assembled Web3 divisions and doubled down on the tech. All of this was scary, but everybody had conviction. They weren't betting on smart contracts, however, or digital assets. They were putting their belief in one another.

As the cars climbed the steep wooden hill and the front passengers curled over the peak, I looked around and remembered that this would be an entirely different experience if I was journeying alone. It certainly wouldn't be as fun and it probably wouldn't have as much meaning. It definitely would have made the ride more scary. I was reminded that I was here for the community, and vice versa. The rollercoaster stood up straight and plunged like an ETH line. From a distance, people couldn't tell the difference between shrieks of terror and howls of laughter. From where I sat, it was all one and the same.

GORDON GONER OF YUGA LABS

If you've heard of NFTs, you're probably thinking of monkey JPEGs. That's because Bored Ape Yacht Club, a ten-thousand-piece NFT collection by Gordon Goner (Wylie Aronow) and Gargamel (Greg Solano) of Yuga Labs, recast the definition in summer 2021. Their collectibles of un-amused monkeys skyrocketed to hundreds of thousands—even millions—of dollars by introducing the expectation of utility around NFTs, a thoughtful road map, a robust community, and also consistent execution. The illustrations also stood out from the rest of the PFP-style art at the time. The unofficial rivalry between BAYC and Crypto-Punks for most expensive floor price took an unexpected turn when Yuga Labs bought CryptoPunks and their ancillary collection, Meebits. Since then, they've introduced their own coin, a metaverse, and continue to acquire other leading projects.

BOBBY: Who were you and what was your life like pre-BAYC? And who are you and what is your life like today?

YUGA: Both of us have always been writers. That hasn't changed. Before we founded Yuga, we both had a love for literature, gaming, and NFTs. We see ourselves as the same storytellers as before—just with a larger platform for creativity and an amazing community supporting us. Before BAYC, I can't say we were throwing parties for more than ten thousand people—so that's definitely new. When we met in our early twenties, we weren't even going to parties. We were more like parking lot kids.

B: What's your elevator pitch on NFTs? How do you define the word "NFT"?

Y: When we talk about NFTs as Yuga sees them, what we're really talking about is two things: authenticity and scarcity. An NFT is a simple piece of technology that allows you to prove ownership on the blockchain—a.k.a., a public ledger. What that means is we can now represent digital items in a way that anyone in the world can verify the origin of that item, and also some cool stuff like how many other items are in that collection. It's an incredibly powerful tool for artists, but also for tons of other use cases, many of which we probably haven't even thought of yet.

BAYC set a new standard for NFT collections, where it was about more than just a unique token or digital art. Your NFT is your key to the club. We think that blending real-world utility with digital ownership is the future of this tech.

B: What's your response to the criticism around NFTs (gambling, Ponzis, etc.)? "NFTs are a scam"?

Y: Anyone that thinks NFTs are a fad doesn't understand the BAYC, CryptoPunks, or Meebits communities. These are thriving communities that act as an online family, whose own tokens come with real-world utility. All over the world, people spend billions of dollars on exclusive memberships, digital and physical events, designer fashion, and more. NFTs aren't any different. They are more than just a digital JPEG that sits in your wallet; they're your ticket to a private concert, exclusive merch drops, and more.

B: BAYC catalyzed the utility and road map components of NFTs, which have become a debated topic in Web3 over the past year. When you were formulating BAYC, was this an intentional play to change the game?

Y: When we started BAYC in 2021, we wanted to stand out from the sea of other projects. We wanted to find a way to do something that was more than just digital art attached to a token. We wanted to find a way to bring storytelling, community, utility, ownership, and decentralization to the forefront of Web3—to build something bigger than just a PFP collection. Our road map, utility, and IP license were a huge part of the collection's initial and sustained success. But I think equally impactful was that we didn't take ourselves too seriously and made something fun and outlandish that we ourselves would want to be part of. Turns out that's a crazy club in the swamp, frequented by apes.

B: In recounting our own journey, I write about how

stressful and anxious it can be for everyone involved around a big project. BAYC has one of the strongest NFT communities, but I'm sure there are instances of tremendous FUD and demands from your holders. Building a Web3 brand is different in this way; everyone's voice does play a part. Can you share some of these fraught moments and how you've dealt with them? What advice do you give Web2 companies who are used to operating autocratically?

Y: Launching a company isn't easy for anyone. We have had our ups and downs as the world of Web3 evolves, but we continue to look to the future. We're so lucky to have such a vocal and passionate community that helps us along the way. I think that community aspect is critical, and something Web2 companies are often missing—we're not just building in public, we're building with the public.

B: At a certain point, it felt like we hit a cap with how many newcomers we were bringing into the space— almost like everyone who would remotely be interested is already here. What sort of cultural milestone, technology, or breakthrough needs to happen in order to bring in the next wave of NFTers, the way we experienced throughout 2021?

Y: We strongly believe that gaming and truly fun experiences will onboard the next one hundred million people into Web3. We're already working on what we see as the next cultural breakthrough: the Otherside metaverse. We've spent the last year making our most ambitious strides toward this goal. We're advancing

the metaverse and reinventing digital ownership unlike ever before, as Otherside will one day be able to be
utilized by anyone. The ultimate plan is for Otherside
to become an open metaverse, where users and assets
can seamlessly transition between different platforms,
worlds, and avatars. This means that Bored Apes, Mu-
tants, Cool Cats, World of Women, and any character
you can think of—including those you create on the
fly, via Otherside's software development kit—are wel-
come in Yuga's metaverse.

B: What's your take on the Metaverse?

Y: Some companies are attempting to build a "metaverse"
that has no compelling reason for people to want to
participate. Legacy tech companies are accustomed to
building in a walled garden where an individual's personal information is the price of admission, and we've
seen how these closed networks exploit the people
that spend time on the services for the benefit of a select few.

In our own approach to Otherside, we thought first
about where we see compelling and long-lasting communities online, and that's in the world of gaming. Our
approach to the Metaverse is an interoperable space
with land, NFTs, tokens, games, and more, to give users the ability to not just participate in new experiences, but to be a creator of experiences and own the
value of those for the community.

B: You've made (yourself and your community) a lot
of money, but I'm sure we are missing what truly
inspires and motivates you to get out of bed and

hammer away at this project every morning. What is driving you and Yuga Labs? What excites you about NFTs?

Y: The BAYC community is what drives us on a daily basis. Our community is constantly creating and inspiring us with innovative ideas and projects. One of the most exciting things to us was granting IP rights to our NFT holders. Seeing what the community is driven to create—from food trucks to films to games and more—has been the most rewarding and fulfilling thing about our jobs.

B: How has the bear market affected your trajectory and plans? Do you ever worry that NFTs will never return to what they were in the bull run?

Y: Not at all. The market is constantly changing—just as traditional markets do—but we are optimistic about the future of NFTs and Web3. The promise of NFTs is that as the world and its spending continue to digitize, it's inherently better for the end user to prove ownership of their digital assets via the blockchain rather than rely on a company's centralized database for them. Game skins you own, instead of ones you rent, for example. More privacy and less user data on a company's server, and so less of a chance for it to be sold off to the highest bidder or hacked into by an authoritarian regime. Easier methods of ensuring provenance and authenticity of luxury goods, with a whole lot less (or zero) middlemen involved. Permissionless settlement layers for transacting with others, lawyers and expensive escrows be damned. We're not there yet, but we think this is a future very much worth building toward.

B: What does the future of NFTs look like?

Y: It will really come down to adoption. We think it's about removing friction for newbies and educating consumers about the opportunities that NFTs and Web3 can bring. We at Yuga feel like we're well on our way to helping make that happen.

EPILOGUE:
NFTS ARE THE FUTURE

Everybody wants to know how the story ends.

Even you. I bet you skipped straight here before completing the book. I'm sure you brushed right over entire chapters (that really hurts my feelings!). You don't have the time or the patience to theorize about metaverse fashion or extrapolate data points on greater-fool tokenomics. All you wanna know is "So, is this thing real or not?" And the answer to that question is . . . almost here.

The internet gave us limitless information and knowledge, but instead of comforting us or making us feel secure with the world, it made us only more unsettled about how ignorant we are. In the immortal lyrics of the legendary East Bay punk band Operation Ivy: "All I know is that I don't know nothing." And the thing that we collectively know the least about is what happens tomorrow. Truly, nothing brings us more fear and worry than the future. While depression is defined as dwelling on the past, anxiety is about being preoccupied with what comes next, the one thing that Google can't clarify or confirm.

Hence, anxiety diagnoses are up worldwide. In the first year of the pandemic, anxiety increased by 25 percent globally. The U.S. Preventive Services Task Force now even recommends all adults be screened for anxiety. And when you observe NFTs and crypto, its most fragile elements are buttressed by a nervous and skittish energy that is perpetually fretting if this is all gonna disappear tomorrow. More than the volatility of the global economy, pervasive scamming, and primitive tech, the main reason why NFTs will fail is our impatience. Meaningful, thoughtful, and sturdy things take time to build, with room to adapt and create along the way to an open destination. It seems like most people in crypto, however, want everything to happen now in a logical fashion that makes sense to them. They want to get rich NOW. They want the tech to operate seamlessly NOW. They want to know how it ends NOW! And they want to hold to a very strict telling of the future to keep any anxiety or worry at bay.

It's like when my kids YouTube a travel destination before we go on vacation. They'd rather bypass the surprise and pull the curtain back on the unknown than sit with anticipation on the flight. My children see the not knowing as an anxious thing, a negative, instead of fun. Whenever I'm in The Hundreds' Discord and I encounter nervous holders who are desperate to know what we're working on, I ask, "This is like asking for details on your surprise party! Don't you want to be caught off guard and amazed?" The answer is no, they don't.*

As a society, we used to be much better about not knowing. It wasn't about being willfully ignorant but being enchanted with curiosity and humbled by puzzlement. One of our mantras at The Hundreds is, "Maintain the Mystery," and it hearkens back to a time when the unknown wasn't something to fix, but a powerful branding tool to storytell around. Since the dawn of time, humans have spoken lore and woven myths to inspire us. These weren't riddles to solve, but stars to guide us. Constellations were spelled out in the sky. We knew we'd never reach them— that wasn't the point. Instead, they were meant to fill us with wonder and a rich creativity.

In the throes of the 2021 NFT bull run, one of the most popular trends was the project road map. Bored Ape Yacht Club was one of the first collections to publish a list of goals they planned to check off on their future agenda. Even though there was not much rational basis for trusting the security of these promises, the road map provided BAYC holders with an artificial sense of safety that their money had been invested in a long-term project (as opposed to a rugpull). Accordingly, other communities pressured their founders to follow suit.

---

* It's easy to complain about today's youth for blurring boundaries, bouncing between different careers, and blending their fashion choices and music tastes, but what that says to me is that they are masters of adaptation. While the older generations prefer the structure and comfort of tradition, they are also having the hardest time adjusting to pandemic protocols, sudden technological advancements, and systemic reform. Meanwhile, young people pivot gracefully between cultural disruptions and other social upheaval.

With Adam Bomb Squad, although we announced some immediate goals for the project, we resisted locking ourselves into a long-term blueprint for the business. For one, we felt that our doxed ownership should be enough to ease people's minds on whether we were gonna ditch the project and run off with people's money. Plus, building a successful, tenured brand over the last couple of decades would surely be enough assurance that we were a safe bet.

The overarching reason we abstained from a road map, however, was that we didn't want to box ourselves in creatively. Two decades ago, when Ben and I started The Hundreds, we didn't write a business plan. If we had, we certainly wouldn't have incorporated NFTs into our future. We didn't wind up in crypto out of design or intention. (I mean, it didn't even exist back then.) Instead, we allowed the brand to foster its own path and personality. Over time, The Hundreds' ethos became centered around community, leading us right into Web3. It happened organically and reinforced the larger brand narrative. Our community wasn't anxious about the journey. They were there to build alongside us, entrusting the team and founders to steward the brand.

To this day, there's still no mission statement for The Hundreds—or Adam Bomb Squad—and when it comes to explaining what it is that we do, it's a long-winded answer. A road map in 2003 would've been relegated to men's T-shirts and baseball caps for the next twenty years. We never imagined that one day we'd run a food festival and be celebrated for our prolific collaborations. We had a footwear program for seven years and opened stores across the country. Today, Ben collects art and is a television host. I'm an author, but also an artist and photographer. Above all, The Hundreds is a streetwear brand that defies genders, genres, age, and classifications. And road maps.*

Adam Bomb Squad and Badam Bomb Squad are NFT collections today, but as NFTs evolve, so will ABS and BBS. Maybe BBS will be used for the food space or cannabis. Perhaps ABS will revolutionize the gaming industry. Adam Bomb is Web3's Mickey Mouse, so we can see him as the central character in an animated series. Personally, I want all these things. To constrain Adam, Badam, and Madam Bomb to static cartoon JPEGs, however, would stunt not just ABS's potential, but what the entire NFT space could become. And then that might really spell the end.

Whenever I get asked if NFTs are a short-lived fad like fidget spinners, I say that I don't think they will die, but they're probably going to be different. NFTs, as we understand them today—as I write about them in this book—will mean something new in the future. They're obviously not going to be million-dollar monkeys forever. Even the word "NFT" is too generalized and clunky and will have to be specifically designated for rightful things. It'd be like if we used the word "MP3" not only for digital music but also for blogs and email in the early 2000s. And, like "MP3," the term "NFT" itself will eventually fade out as the technol-

* In my favorite movie, *Back to the Future*, Christopher Lloyd's character, Doc Brown, tells Marty McFly, "Roads? Where we're going, we don't need roads!"

ogy becomes more ubiquitous and ingrained in our daily lives.

Already, in the last one to two years, much of what I've written about has changed. When CryptoPunks ruled the roost, they were 8-bit art with no expectation of utility. Once the Bored Apes entered, an NFT wasn't legitimate unless it provided useful value beyond the JPEG alone. Today, utility is once again being reconsidered (even the requisite road map's become a thing of the past). In May 2022, an anonymously run, ten-thousand-piece NFT collection called Goblintown successfully minted out, with the floor price rapidly climbing to 4 ETH ($4,800 at the time). The project captured the mood of the bear market crash at the time, with their Twitter Spaces town halls conducted with inaudible grunts and an NFT.NYC party that was sheer mayhem. Most interesting of all, Goblintown's success was founded on none of the principles that had been professed as truth. Their website proudly proclaimed, "No road map. No Discord. No utility. CC0." Beeple called it "a shockingly low effort pump and dump project" and yet the project has achieved almost 60,000 ETH ($78,416,400.00 at the time of this writing) in sales volume.

As mentioned, there's a war waging in the background surrounding marketplaces and royalties. If the tides eventually turn against the artists in this way, it'll be a detour in everyone's road maps that they never expected. But out of survival and ingenuity, the artists, founders, and creators will adapt once again and either disrupt the existing technology or forge a new one. What does it mean for Adam Bomb Squad holders if the NFT experience, as we appreciate it today, is fleeting? It'll just mean that they'll be reborn as something better that we can't picture now. That's exactly how and why Web3 began.

Just two years ago, almost every person in the NFT space was doing something else. In some of my NFT chats, we have rock stars and social media influencers, artists, writers, and lawyers. One day, like dinosaurs oblivious to the meteor heading toward our planet, we were broadsided by Web3 and nothing's been the same since. What else awaits us in this life, ready to upend our realities and worldviews? What new technology is currently being concocted in a lab that can change our world? We didn't see NFT 1.0 coming. We're certainly unprepared for NFT 2.0. I can guarantee you, however, that it will be real and we will meet the challenge with courage and a boundless imagination. When only half of Americans own crypto and less than a quarter know what an NFT is, everything that's happened until now is merely primer. If you missed out, now couldn't be a better time to dive in. This isn't how the story ends, but rather, how it begins.

Or am I getting ahead of myself?

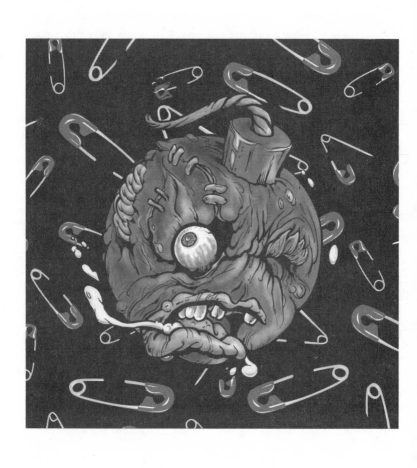

FREQUENTLY ASKED QUESTIONS

What's an NFT?

The far too simple answer:

An NFT is a digital record (think certificate or receipt) on the blockchain (what's a blockchain?; see next) that you own something. That "something" can be digital, but it can also be physical (like a concert ticket). A common misconception is that the term "NFT" means the actual object or asset. It's like conflating a deed with the house. Although they are two separate things, for simplicity's sake, "NFT" is used interchangeably with the associated product.

An NFT can be:

Art (the easiest way to understand NFTs. Art simplifies complicated ideas. This is why artists are always on the frontlines of cultural progression)

A membership card (the most practical application, like a loyalty rewards program or pass to a social club)

A trading card (a novelty collectible like a sports card or Pokémon card)

An investment like a stock (in fact, most of the above already behave like a stock)

Many of the NFTs in popular culture (like a Bored Ape) are a combination of all the above.

In sum, the NFT is the contract that declares you are the one and only owner of that thing.

Wait, what's the blockchain?

Picture a string of computers around the world universally agreeing on business transactions that are happening over the network. They must all be on the same page to record the transaction and it would take all of them to agree to edit it. Thus, the record is immutable—it can't be edited—and is therefore considered the truth. The defining feature of blockchain technology is that the data is distributed across multiple computers, making it decentralized. There is no central administrator—no authoritative figure, government, or corporation—in charge.

Blockchain technology was invented for the first and most prominent cryptocurrency, Bitcoin. Since then, technologists have realized the blockchain can have many other uses, like smart contracts that automatically release payments once a contract's been fulfilled.

In 2013, two developers named Vitalik Buterin and Gavin Wood authored the Ethereum blockchain, which became the most popular blockchain to support NFTs. Other blockchains that people use to trade NFTs include Polygon (MATIC), Solana (SOL), Tezos (XTZ), and Avalanche (AVAX).

Where do I begin investing in NFTs if I've never bought before (we have crypto)?

You need three things to create and/or buy NFTs:

1. Crypto. Ether (ETH) is the cryptocurrency used in the Ethereum platform. It is also the mainstream cryptocurrency for NFTs. You can buy ETH on an exchange like Coinbase. Since crypto is decentralized—meaning there's no middleman—you become the bank.

2. A "hot" wallet. On a desktop computer, sign up for a MetaMask wallet. Move ETH from your crypto exchange (like Coinbase) into your wallet, and then plug your wallet into online marketplaces like OpenSea to shop for NFTs. (Use Google Chrome and download the plug-in for MetaMask on your browser.)

3. For safety reasons, you should also have a "cold" wallet like Ledger. Cold wallets store your crypto and NFTs on physical devices that look like a USB drive. This protects you online from hackers or from your own careless mistakes (e.g., clicking on the wrong link and getting your hot wallet drained by a bad actor. This happens a lot!).

You can buy NFTs directly when they drop on their own websites, but the most popular ones sell out immediately. Therefore, most NFT purchases are done on the secondary market (think eBay and StockX). This is harder to understand for an older generation who understood secondhand goods as "used." It's a bit easier for collectors who've traded sneakers over resale sites or trade vintage clothing. With NFTs, however, the original creator continues to receive royalties forever on every secondary sale. The most popular auction exchange for NFTs is OpenSea, but there's also Coinbase NFT, LooksRare, X2Y2, and a slew of others. Have fun and choose wisely!

How are you dealing with the backlash to NFTs? Critics who claim it's a scam or cynics who believe it's a short-lived fad?

I agree that much of the NFT, Web3, and Metaverse discussion is confusing, if not bewildering. A lot of it is admittedly stupid or scammy. Some of it, I agree, is scary.

I try to be gentle with the doubters and critics because we're living in a time of great transition. Most of us just want the ground to stop shaking before we're forced to enter a virtual existence where JPEGs cost thousands of dollars.

It will take time. For some people, that time will never come. We all have friends who never signed on to Web2 (blogs, social media) and were perfectly happy without it. The same will hold true for Web3. It's not for everybody and if it's not for you, that's okay.

What can the Metaverse be used for beyond video games? Why do we need it? For example, could a cannabis dispensary work in the Metaverse?

As wild as it sounds, all physical retail has a functional home in the Metaverse. In my opinion, the entire internet is already the Metaverse, even if it doesn't visually parallel what you see in the physical world. It's almost like we're still in that green grid of zeros and ones in the Matrix, without all the fancy exterior dressed on top.

The Postmates and DoorDash apps are metaverses, except a skeletal wireframe of text and drop-down menus. Imagine purchasing a product in a virtual venue instead—a beautifully designed digital storefront—and then the product (food, clothing, or weed!) is delivered to your door. It's a much more appealing user experience than buying food off a sterile menu. Also, if you're already spending time in this specific metaverse environment (for social or gaming reasons), why leave to order off a delivery app? Do it from within the digital space, with your friends, and with more context to what you're ordering than merely fonts and static photos.

If I don't have a lot of money to spare, should I invest in crypto?

In my opinion, no.

You should only play with money you can afford to lose.

Our world is becoming more unpredictable with violent swings between trends. This applies not only to politics and cultural attitudes but to investment opportunities. These days, you can make money fast, but it can disappear faster. So you must be prepared to wake up with zero in your account without warning.

This is not financial advice.

Can NFTs help a small family business like mine?

NFTs can be for anyone who is wrestling with a problem

and sees an opportunity for the technology to facilitate or expedite a solution.

Do your research and fully grasp the tech and philosophy around Web3 and NFTs, from the blockchain to smart contracts and decentralization. If you don't see an inroads for your business, NFTs might not be there yet for you.

NFTs are not the answer in themselves. They are the tool. *You* are the answer. You are the genius craftsman, not the hammer.

For two decades, we've been trying to figure out how to give our community true sense of ownership in a brand and for the first time, we're seeing those avenues emerge because of Web3.

Diagnose the problem. Find the best technology to help you fix it. If it doesn't exist, make it or wait for it. It'll come.

Will NFTs and Web3 collapse? This reminds me of the dot-com bubble.

Absolutely. Ninety-nine percent of NFT projects will fail, change, or evolve with time. We've already seen some of the leading projects and celebrated founders quietly vanish over the years. We are in the nascent stages of technology and it'd be foolish to believe this is how it's going to be forever.

With regards to Web3 and the Metaverse, however, the presentation may change, but the perspective will stay. Especially when it comes to blockchain technology, decentralization, and smart contracts. I staunchly believe these will be fundamental for future industries.

Remember: We are in the primitive, early days of this

new world. Try to keep an open mind to what it could be and where it can go. Don't focus on the clunky metaverse graphics or childish NFT avatars. These are stepping stones to a destination (better metaverse graphics will require Herculean servers that are still being built in the background). I know this doesn't make sense—but if social media had been around when the internet first fired up, the world would've collectively laughed at—and attempted to cancel—the raw coded interfaces and AOL mail before them.

In the West, we have cultivated a dystopian sense of technology, but remember—in other parts of the world, tech has saved and improved many lives. Consider that new tech can be a powerful and positive force.

What would be different if you ran the Metaverse, not Mark Zuckerberg?

Unfortunately, there's a misconception out there that the Metaverse is the same as Meta, Mark Zuckerberg's Facebook rebrand. This is not true. The cleanest definition of the Metaverse is an immersive digital environment that uses a combination of virtual reality (VR) and augmented reality (AR) to blur the boundaries with the physical world. Although this has already been in the works over the last couple of decades, especially in the gaming sector, the term "Metaverse" adds an interoperable ownership component. This means that the assets you own in a video game or on a social media platform can be utilized in other programs. For example, your Nike NFT that you bought from the Nike corporation should also be able to be worn in *Fortnite*, which is owned by Epic Games.

My personal definition of the Metaverse is a little looser. The Metaverse is the moment—even if brief and intermittent—where our consciousness and experiences in the digital and physical worlds become indiscernible. Under this meaning, we are constantly diving in and out of the Metaverse in modern life. Many of our conversations with friends are digitally bound, much of our work life exists online.

The Metaverse is comprised of many individual metaverses, who should be open to collaborating and conversing with one another in the true spirit of decentralization. Zuck is working on his own metaverse (called Meta), but there are many others out there like Sandbox, Decentraland, and some.place.

If I ran Zuck's Meta, I would ensure that it plays nicely with other metaverse companies and also shares ownership fairly with its constituents. To many NFTers, Zuck's project goes against the ethos of Web3, which is where the community is empowered and enriched, not just Mark.

I keep hearing how terrible NFTs are for the environment—is this true?

Like any manmade product in the world, of course, energy is required to make NFTs. Just like the TikTok servers are churning for you to view a dance video. Like the hamburger you ate for dinner purged methane into the air. Like the car you drove to work in, or the plane you traveled across the ocean in, brushed fuel across the earth.

Although NFTs are a small percentage of energy use in crypto, the computers mining the Ether used to demand a great deal of electricity. How much is debatable, but regardless, environmentally friendlier advancements have been made across the technology. There are green Bitcoin mining companies like Terawulf being built. And as of September 2022, the Ethereum merge upgraded the system to a proof-of-stake validation (versus proof-of-work), reducing its carbon emissions by nearly 100 percent. (Chains like Tezos and Solana, meanwhile, have already been implementing this.) That means using the Ethereum network requires a bare fraction of the energy that watching YouTube or Netflix does.

Even still, there is the potential for NFTs to alleviate waste across other sectors as well. For example, instead of using gas to drive and meet someone, we can reduce the carbon footprint by meeting in a metaverse. Or, we can make fewer physical things if the emotional components of the purchase can be substituted with a digital product. The best illustration of this is fashion.

According to a 2020 World Economic Forum report, "fashion production makes up 10% of humanity's carbon emissions, dries up water sources, and pollutes rivers and streams. What's more, 85% of all textiles go to the dump each year. And washing some types of clothes sends thousands of bits of plastic into the ocean."

We already have enough clothing, so people buy fashion today for identity, community, and ownership. Digital wearables can provide all these effects and simultaneously reduce fashion's carbon footprint. No polluting factories, shipping and airing, harmful oils and chemicals, dirtied water, landfills, etc. Just great art and design.

How can I as a small brand get into NFTs?

Know the rules, then break 'em.

Understand the space and players, identify what is missing or inefficient, then define how you can address these issues. What makes your idea different, disruptive, and inspiring?

Small brands have the greatest advantage in NFTs because much of Web3 logic goes against the architecture of larger corporations. In fact, I believe bigger businesses will continue to stumble and fail at Web3 while independent brands will be able to adapt quicker and hand the keys over to their communities.

Why does it seem like Web3 leaders are the same rich white leaders from Web2?

Because many are. Especially if you're seeing the same VC model play out again, with the same tired start-ups and tech founders of yesteryear repackaging themselves as Web3 players.

There's an even bigger manipulation happening as well.

You see how difficult and confusing it is to get into NFTs, right? That's intentional.

The information is purposefully asymmetrical, gatekept by individuals who speak tech and finance, two subjects that have historically been passed down through certain clubs only.

They don't want you in.

They don't want you to win.

They don't want you to threaten their power.

Unfortunately for them, they won't be able to withhold the information much longer.

The models are designed to topple oligarchies.

There are too many of us already in.

And we are out there onboarding our communities in droves.

Let's. Go.

Are we heading toward *Ready Player One*?

Check your screen time on your phone today.

I think we're already here.

Will the Metaverse cancel out social media or will we use both?

I see many people think Web3 is a zero-sum game. Like, because of the Metaverse, humans will stop going outside. Or if NFTs get popular, society will stop supporting physical art.

I see it the other way. I've bought more physical paintings this year because NFTs have heightened my universal awareness of art. I spend a certain amount of time online as it is, so instead of boring Zooms or flat email correspondence, I'd much rather build with people in a fun and expressive digital environment.

Not only can everything coexist, life and experiences can get better because of NFTs and the Metaverse.

What's the goofiest thing you've experienced in NFTs/Web3?

Ha. There's a lot.

It's hard to judge, however, if people are sincerely and

honestly trying to figure it out. Not only can I not knock them for that, I appreciate the effort. It's like the early black-and-white footage of the first airplanes with flapping wings, catching on fire. I'm sure the planes looked just as ridiculous at the time, but these inventors were committed to a dream and an answer. We wouldn't have gotten the airplanes of today without the goofy shit.

Are NFTs a fad?
Maybe. I have no idea.

Although I don't embark on much without longevity in mind, you never know what's gonna happen tomorrow.

In the pandemic, I didn't know I'd run into NFTs. They changed my career. They changed my life.

But if you step further back, at the start of 2020, I didn't know I'd run into a pandemic. It changed my career; it changed my life.

I have no idea what's gonna happen five years from now, ten years, or one hundred. And that's also why as doubtful as I am of the future, I'm confident that Adam Bomb Squad will be alive and well.

Because, why not? Anything can happen.

Baseline requirements for success for an NFT project?
You have to care.

You have to be curious.

You have to be a part of the community.

Any part of you that is disheartened or wary about the Metaverse?
I know this sounds crazy, but no.

I'm really excited about it.

I feel like we spend all this time on the internet in largely unappealing, ugly interfaces.

If we're going to engage online—whether it's on Zoom calls, or Slack channels, or Adobe programs—why not design the worlds and ourselves to be more interesting?

I have the utmost faith in the technology and the people who are building in the background. Through this process, I've met some of the smartest and most visionary people in the world. The brightest brains and the best intentions are applying themselves to see this through.

Also, there's no COVID in the Metaverse. Win.

NFTs seem expensive and unattainable.

The NFTs you see in popular media are prohibitively expensive for most people on the planet. Like all things you read in the news, look beyond the sensational headlines to the real stories.

NFTs can range in price from free (we give out free POAPs every week on my live talk show) to a million dollars. There are NFTs that are the cost of a physical T-shirt. There's art on some chains that's, like, $20. There are Adam Bomb Squad NFTs that are—on the cheap end—about a few hundred bucks. Although this is on the lower level for an Ethereum-based NFT project, I understand that seems like a lot of money to many who aren't in the NFT space. Yet many Adam Bomb Squad holders would say it's totally worth it for the community, brand perks, social badge, and access that the bomb provides.

If I were to tell you a car cost $1,000, you might say that sounds reasonable. But if I were to say a JPEG cost $1,000, it might seem unconscionable. For many NFT collectors, however, the $1,000 JPEG has more utility, meaning, and profitability on resale than a car would.

Just as some people reading this would sneer at a $500 pair of Nikes, most of my audience doesn't see much wrong with it. Hard to judge . . . So relative value is everything here.

TLDR—I don't know what any of this means!

You've been conditioned to believe that everything on the other side of the screen should be free. Even in the early 2000s with blogs, the nature of right-click-saving someone's photography felt unnatural and inherently wrong. At the time, we Photoshopped watermarks on images in a futile attempt to claim them. Then, we gave up.

Over time, because of social media, we relinquished ownership of our digital content. The social media giants convinced you that your pictures and captions were free and democratized, for all to enjoy.

But your creation—what they reclassified as "content"—always had an owner. It was Facebook or Google or whomever. And your content had a monetary value. It's what the tech companies sold to advertisers for eyeballs and clicks.

We're finally waking up to—and remembering—the truth that everything online was created by someone and that creator should be compensated fairly for their work. Just like it is in the physical world, the same should be for the digital.

ACKNOWLEDGMENTS

The last two years have been the most trying years of my life and I couldn't have gotten through them without the following and their support:

God.

Misa, your patience, grace, and steadfast faith in us make the impossible possible. I feel superhuman because of you. Thank you for letting me get swept away, no matter how stormy the seas.

Kalen and Barrett, I watched you become young men in the process of writing this book. Pondering the future was easy because you're always on my mind.

Ben, for lending me your ear and full attention. In those first few weeks I discovered NFTs (and couldn't stop babbling like a crazy person), you threw your entire everything behind the possibility. To believing each other and believing in each other.

Sandy Mosqueda, David Rivera, Joey Gonzales, and The Hundreds. You make the work worthwhile and my life full. You've taught me so much. Sometimes I think my job is an excuse just to hang out with you as much as I can.

My friends and comrades in this space are too many

to list. My God, you've saved me so many times. A special shout-out to the homies in Seed Round, $0.15, Legends Only, Chad Team 6, OK SO, Surfers, DAO Jones, and CPG for partying with me in hell.

Adam Bomb Squad. What can I say? To the best Community on Planet Earth, the ones who've held since mint, the leaders who've given us their all, and even the FUDders we've lost along the way. Your belief and participation make it meaningful. Without you, NFTs would be such a scam!

Sonia Nikore. You've walked the entire journey with me and never let go of my hand. Thank you for guiding me with care and compassion.

Sean McDonald and Marc Gerald, that's two for two. Once again, you took a chance on me, and I hope the bet is fruitful. That's some strong conviction!

Finally, to you, the reader. A book would just be words on pages if you weren't there to appreciate them. When I write, I imagine the text flowing like a conversation, and therefore I try to consider as much of your voice and insight in the process as possible. I hope you see yourself in the work.

Thank you.

A NOTE ABOUT THE AUTHOR

Bobby Kim, also known as Bobby Hundreds, is the author of *This Is Not a T-Shirt*. He is an illustrator, a documentarian, a designer, and a writer. In 2003, he cofounded The Hundreds, a global men's streetwear brand and editorial platform, with Ben Shenassafar and a few hundred bucks. The two are also partners in Second Sons, a brand-development group that incubates, structures, and facilitates other small businesses. Hundreds lives in Los Angeles with his wife and two sons.